MAINTAINING MOMENTUM

PROMOTING SOCIAL MOBILITY AND LIFE CHANCES FROM EARLY YEARS TO ADULTHOOD

EDITED BY SIMONE DELORENZI, JODIE REED
AND PETER ROBINSON

The ippr

The Institute for Public Policy Research (ippr) is the UK's leading progressive think tank and was established in 1988. Its role is to bridge the political divide between the social democratic and liberal traditions, the intellectual divide between academia and the policy making establishment and the cultural divide between government and civil society. It is first and foremost a research institute, aiming to provide innovative and credible policy solutions. Its work, the questions its research poses and the methods it uses are driven by the belief that the journey to a good society is one that places social justice, democratic participation and economic and environmental sustainability at its core.

For further information you can contact ippr's external affairs department on info@ippr.org, you can view our website at www.ippr.org and you can buy our books from Central Books on 0845 458 9910 or email ippr@centralbooks.com.

Our trustees

© ippr 2005
Typeset by Emphasis

CONTENTS

Preface

Social mobility has a number of different definitions and dimensions. To sociologists, it refers to the movement or opportunities for movement between different social groups – with a particular focus on the role (or otherwise) of social class in acting as a barrier to such movement. To economists, it refers to the movement or opportunities for movement between different income groups – with a particular focus on the extent to which children's incomes are correlated with those of their parents.

Social mobility can also be considered over one's own life time (intra-generational mobility) or between generations of one's family (inter-generational mobility).

What has been happening to social mobility depends considerably on the definition and timescale one considers, as work by the Strategy Unit has found[1]. Looking over the last century, and taking into account the substantial expansion in the number of professional, managerial and administrative jobs and the corresponding decline in manual jobs, the 'middle class' has grown enormously compared with the 'working class' and this has permitted equally substantial *numbers* of people in Britain to enjoy upward social mobility.

If on the other hand one focuses on recent decades, the correlation between parents' and children's incomes appears to have risen over time – suggesting falling inter-generational social mobility. Intra-generational income mobility also appears to have declined in recent decades. And, even over the longer term, the comparative *chances* of people from different social backgrounds making it to a particular social position seem to have changed relatively little.

What is happening to social mobility matters for both economic and social reasons. A country's economic performance, and individuals' capacity to better themselves and their families, will be undermined if social class or other barriers prevent them from making the best use of their talents and skills. Lack of social mobility implies inequality of opportunity.

On the other hand, equality of opportunity/social mobility is only one dimension of social justice. Fairness of outcomes, including the absence of poverty, may be another concern of policymakers. Evidence suggests both will determine individuals' life chances and quality of life amongst other factors. Equality of opportunity and fairness of outcomes aren't necessarily in conflict – as Gosta Esping-Anderson's paper in this volume argues – but, in principle at least, high levels of social mobility could co-exist with poverty amongst those who, for whatever reason, aren't upwardly mobile.

1 Social Mobility – A Discussion Paper, April 2001; Life Chances and Social Mobility – An Overview of the Evidence, March 2004

The challenge for governments and policymakers is then both to establish the appropriate balance between interventions to promote equality of opportunity and social mobility and interventions to promote fairer outcomes, wherever there is potential conflict between them, and also to identify the mix of interventions that is likely to be most effective in achieving their social justice and other goals.

The former is likely ultimately to require a political judgment. The latter, to which this report makes a particular contribution, requires research and evaluation evidence. As individuals' life chances have multiple drivers a mix of different policy interventions is likely to be needed to achieve policy goals. But what is or should be the preferred mix?

This publication helps us understand what is happening to opportunity and social mobility and to trends in poverty and incomes – in Britain and other countries – and why. It also provides an invaluable synthesis of the evidence on the effectiveness of interventions such as parental leave, childcare, parenting support, early years' education, schooling and labour market interventions.

Stephen Aldridge
Acting Director of the Strategy Unit
writing solely in a personal capacity
January 2005

1 Introduction
Simone Delorenzi, Jodie Reed and Peter Robinson

This report brings together the substantive papers that were presented at the Social Mobility and Life Chances Forum that took place on 3 – 4 December 2004, as well as reflecting on the issues and themes that were discussed in the many sessions that took place during the Forum. The ippr owes a great debt to the authors of these papers and to the many other colleagues who made presentations at the event, took part in panel discussions or contributed to the debates that took place. It also owes a great debt to the organisations whose support enabled the event to take place: the Sutton Trust, CfBT and the Barrow Cadbury Trust.

The sub-title of the 2004 Forum was 'maintaining momentum' which in this context has a two-fold meaning. This event was the third in a series that was kicked off in September 2003 with a conference that brought together a wide range of people and was addressed by the Chancellor Gordon Brown. This was followed up by a well-attended seminar held at HM Treasury in March 2004. The third event was therefore maintaining the momentum in a series that has allowed participants to step back and think through the implications for public policy of a focus on improving social mobility and life chances. Many of the same colleagues have attended all three events and have therefore been able to see how various lines of argument have evolved, although this third seminar also involved a lot of new participants including several colleagues from the US and the EU.

However, the main reason for choosing the sub-title 'maintaining momentum' was to encourage colleagues to focus on the important question of how to prioritise the range of interventions which across the life cycle might improve individuals' life chances and their social mobility. Previous events had given emphasis to the importance of interventions in the early years in helping to break down the link between people's social origins and their destinations as adults. Indeed part of the agenda for this third event was to test just how solid the consensus was on the importance and the precise parameters of the early years agenda.

However, there had always been a recognition that the gains made in children's development through early interventions might not be sustained without further interventions, during the period of compulsory schooling and as adults enter the labour market and later on during their lives. The question then was how to maintain the momentum towards more equal life chances and improved social mobility for the disadvantaged through policy interventions that built on what might be achieved through policies relating to the early years.

A summary of the seminar presentations and discussion is available at www.ippr.org/ research/ socialpolicy/beyond activewelfare.

This focus on the range of policy interventions immediately raises the key question of how we prioritise the allocation of scarce public resources across different areas of public policy. Previous events had begun to home in on this issue of whether the evidence base allowed policy makers to make clear judgments about where to deploy the 'marginal pound' to best effect in order to enhance life chances and promote social mobility. This question is becoming all the more urgent because public resources are about to become all the more scarce. After 2006–7 the rate of growth in public spending is being reigned back again following a period of quite rapid increases in expenditure which has allowed the government to fire on all fronts in its attempts to reduce relative poverty and to provide enhanced public services. This reigning in will require policy makers to be all the more discerning in where they deploy extra resources to best effect.

The immediate back-drop to the December 2004 Forum illustrated very clearly the key theme that will echo through this report, of how to marry enormous ambition with limited resources. The emerging consensus, at least among policy elites, around the importance of the early years agenda, a consensus that this series of events has played some modest role in helping to cement, was reflected in the government's ten-year strategy for childcare published the day before the Forum. At the same time the first stages of that strategy were put in place through announcements made in the 2004 Pre-Budget Report. However, only £600 million of new funding by 2007–8 was committed to this new leg of the welfare state, far short of the levels of expenditure typical in countries such as Sweden or Denmark which are held up as the paragons in this area of public policy.

The event on the 3 and 4 December 2004 was organised in two broad sessions. The first day focussed on the early years and on schooling and the second day on the economy and on the labour market and the distribution of income and wealth. This split is also reflected in this summary chapter, which gives an overview of some of the main discourses emerging from the Forum including papers published in this volume and other contributions not included in this collection. We start with the debate over the early years as the new leg of the welfare state.

Early Years: Building from emerging consensus?

Despite decades of effort since the end of the second world war to increase social mobility through education, the life chances of individuals in the UK today are still heavily determined by their social origins. Comprehensive schools, which were intended to put children from all backgrounds on an equal footing, have not brought about the expected changes: the kind of occupation and income that an adult will reach in the labour market are still heavily dependent on their parents' own level of achievement and income.

Gosta Esping-Andersen argues in his chapter that this is because life chances are heavily determined by the development of cognitive abilities between birth and six years, that is mainly before children even start school. And these cognitive abilities are most dependent on parents' cultural capital, their ability to engage in stimulating activities and to impart attitudes and motivation that will pay dividends in the school years and later in life. The only countries which have managed to significantly reduce the determinism of social inheritance are the Scandinavian countries, especially Sweden. Esping-Andersen puts this down to high quality and universal childcare and early years education, which reduce the role of the family milieu children are born into and produce higher levels of social mobility.

However, high quality childcare and early years services for all from twelve months until school begins, with well qualified staff, comes at a significant cost. Sweden spends about two per cent of its GDP on early years provision compared to about half a per cent in Britain. Despite the wider social gains mentioned by Esping-Andersen, high quality universal early years provision will always carry with it a heavy net cost to the taxpayer. This cost has to be balanced against the costs of other interventions and the whole panoply of services the welfare state provides.

It also has to be acknowledged that early childhood services cannot be considered in isolation from their wider welfare and political contexts (Moss, 2004). The Scandinavian model is strongly related to specific social and political values, such as a commitment to equality and democracy, which explains its success. Whether it can be replicated simply through transposing it to a much larger, less homogeneous country such as Britain is highly debatable.

Jane Waldfogel shows in her chapter that if there is an important role for early childhood education, there is no single magic bullet for improving the life chances of individuals. There is a role for other policies as well, and all policies imply trade offs between the gains they are meant to achieve and their side effects. For example, increased parental leave is considered most beneficial for the mother's and the child's health as well as for the child's cognitive and social and emotional development. However, it can have costs in terms of the negative repercussions on the careers of women taking extra leave and therefore on gender equity. These kinds of trade offs need to be explicitly recognised if we want to develop public policies that do not achieve improvements in some areas at the expense of others. Promoting social inclusion, reducing child poverty, increasing parental employment in low-income families, supporting parental choice and promoting gender equity are all important and inter-related outcomes that need to be balanced.

A wide range of policies need to be considered in order to tackle different causes of social disadvantage with different remedies at successive stages.

In research that has had significant influence on the development of the government's ten-year strategy for childcare, Jane Waldfogel has advocated a range of policies throughout childhood. This starts with an extension of paid parental leave in the infant's first year; high-quality centre-based care for children up to two years old, starting with the most disadvantaged; and the development of a more integrated system of high-quality care and pre-school education for those between three and five years. In the ten-year strategy announced in December 2004, the government committed itself to an extension of parental leave from six to nine months, the option to transfer some leave to fathers and more free nursery education for three to four-year olds.

The need for joined up services is another aspect of provision which currently attracts a wide consensus at the political level and was extensively discussed at the Forum. Families are to be given access to a wide range of programmes through teams that work collaboratively to make sure that all the needs they identify are responded to. An example in Britain are Sure Start Children's Centres, where families in deprived areas can find early education, childcare, child and maternal health services, family advice and employment guidance. The government's ten-year strategy set out to expand the network of centres to 3,500 by the end of the decade. However, without sufficient funds to allow the programme to expand along the lines of the initial model, this is deemed as the dismantling of the project in all but name by one of its initiators (Norman Glass, 2005). Two key dimensions of the Sure Start programme are likely to give way: the integration of health services and community participation in programme development. Joined up services are difficult to sustain without relatively generous funding. If the jam is spread too thinly, programmes tend to concentrate on the most cost-effective minimal core, which in this case is likely to mean childcare of diverse quality.

The home learning environment, that is learning activities which parents engage in, such as reading with their children, has a stronger impact on later attainment in school than either the mother's qualification level or the family socio-economic status (Sammons, 2004). However, children who do not attend childcare centres before going to school have poorer attainments at school than those who do, particularly in terms of language development and social behaviour. Disadvantaged children benefit most from centre-based care. But this depends a lot on the quality and duration of pre-school provision. Research has shown that children make most progress in their cognitive and social behavioural development when they are attended to by highly qualified staff. The very well regarded childcare provision in Scandinavia is provided by well-paid staff, with at least three years of training. If childcare is to be the priority the government wants, more resources need to be put into training and retaining a skilled workforce. Creative strategies also need to be devised to attract more people into the profession, targeting a wider pool that should include more over 50s and be less focused on young women.

Parenting support programmes have aroused wide interest in recent years. They have been burgeoning through numerous public, private and voluntary initiatives and organisations. There are very sound reasons for this: as mentioned above, parenting has been shown to be the most important factor in the child's cognitive development and well-being. However, there are limits to the extent to which parenting interventions can improve life chances (Edwards, 2004). Even if we can describe accurately 'poor parenting' as well as an 'optimum' style of parenting, intervening to increase the prevalence of 'good parenting' is not straightforward. Intervening in how parents' parent is different from defining what good parenting means: it is a much more personal intervention and can be seen as difficult and intrusive. It also carries the risk of stigmatising specific people, such as poor parents or single mothers, who are most likely to be targeted if the system could not afford to be universal.

Among the myriad of parenting programmes that are on offer, those which seem to bring most benefits are structured and targeted programmes with clear objectives and trained staff, in a combination of centre activities and home visits. However, overall evaluation remains patchy and inconclusive, not least because of the plethora of small scale initiatives. On the current base of knowledge therefore, parental support programmes may not be the most cost-effective type of intervention and the focus now should be on doing further research.

There is a general consensus amongst policy makers that there is a need to spend more in the early years to improve the life chances of individuals. There is also agreement on a range of policies that need to be implemented, as the congruence between leading researchers and the government's ten-year strategy made clear. But as yet there is no popular consensus and maybe even some concern that the childless will not support further significant resources being transferred to families with children.

Maintaining momentum through the school years

The recent focus on early years policies does not mean that only the first years of children's lives are important. If the efforts made at the start are not sustained, their positive effects may fade away by the time children finish their second year of compulsory schooling. The EPPE Research (Effective Provision of Pre-School Education) shows that some of the benefits provided by pre-school care in terms of cognitive and social behavioural developments are still perceptible by the end of Key Stage 1 (insofar as tests can be assumed to reflect attainment) (Sylva et al., 2004). The momentum gained through early years is therefore maintained to a certain degree into the first stage of primary school. But it may fade away in following years. While such longitudinal research is not yet available up to secondary years, international comparisons (OECD's Programme for International Student Assessment(PISA)) are unpromising in this regard. They show that although Britain's fifteen year olds score well on average in tests in mathematics, science and literacy, the UK is one of the countries with the strongest association between pupils' socio-economic background and their school performance (Schümer, 2004).

Schools alone cannot change the life course so heavily determined by initial social inequities. Even in favourable conditions, middle class children continue to outperform working class children. However, attending an effective school can still have a major impact on the life chances of disadvantaged students.

In their chapter, Alice Sullivan and Geoff Whitty argue that the quality of teachers is the most important factor in accounting for the differences in achievement. Small classes can play a role too, but only if substantial reductions are made in disadvantaged areas, as opposed to reductions that are thinly spread across all schools.

The specific school a child attends is important not only because it determines aspects of provision such as class sizes, teaching and learning and the kind of teachers it will be able to attract, but also because of composition or peer group effects. If children from disadvantaged backgrounds all attend the same schools, these effects can lead to low overall attainment. International comparisons show that an even social mix of pupils leads to better average results, mainly through better results for the disadvantaged.

However, the government's continuation of policies introduced by the Conservatives aimed at emphasising choice of schools by parents means there has been little change in de facto social segregation between schools. Middle class parents have more economic and cultural resources allowing them to effectively put their children in the schools of their choice. Whether these schools are intrinsically more effective in their teaching and learning or not, the mere fact that different social classes are segregated is negative in terms of global outcomes and tackling socio-economic inequalities.

It has been argued that the other side of the government's strategy, the promotion of an education quasi-market through school autonomy and competition via league tables, reinforces polarisation. With the existing admissions system schools choose children as much as parents choose schools. Indeed, as more schools are encouraged to take on Foundation status thereby becoming their own admissions authority this situation may be reinforced. To promote a better social mix, admission policies might need to be made more transparent and standardised.

According to the Department for Education and Skills' five-year strategy for children and learners, all schools are to become extended schools, offering study support activities, facilities for community activities and family learning. However, it is far from clear how this is to be reconciled with the concept of school autonomy: there is no guarantee that, in a competing world, all schools will sign up to the idea of schools in the community.

The concept of extended schools responds to the same basic principles around which Sure Start Children's Centres have been conceived. Joined up services are to be accessed from the same central location and local communities are to be consulted in order to foster a sense of ownership and to make sure that programmes respond to local needs. Children's Trusts will have responsibility for developing this system to ensure continuity throughout childhood and into the teenage years. However, in line with the arguments around Sure Start, the strategy of delivering universal provision through Children's Trusts and devolving control to local authorities is perceived as high risk. It could lead to a loss of community focus and to a spread of resources that would mean that deprived communities which need the services most might not benefit as much as with more targeted provision.

The year on year rise in the number of pupils gaining a good batch of higher grade GCSEs is positive in terms of social mobility, as achieving a good qualification at sixteen is the best predictor of achievement at A-level and later in the labour market. However, it does not necessarily mean an improvement in social justice terms, as the association between social class and educational achievement remains significant. With this in mind, the reduction of the National Curriculum at Key Stage 4 and greater choice pre and post 16 might reinforce segregation. In a system where there is no 'parity of esteem' between the vocational and academic routes, it is not the better-informed middle class children who are most likely to take up vocational options, which have less purchasing power in higher education institutions and the labour market. The widely held assumption that vocational courses are the best solution for under-achievers also means that they are generally seen as being solely for under-achievers (Steer, 2004). Maybe the current focus on introducing work-based or vocational courses into Key Stage 4 and beyond should be replaced by more creative strategies focusing on teaching of generic applied skills.

Gender, race and ethnicity are important dimensions of the social mobility debate. However, the educational achievement of minority ethnic pupils is often strongly correlated with that of social class. As for gender, the fact that girls tend to outperform boys should not be considered as a major issue at this stage, considering the wider disadvantages facing girls when making choices regarding their careers and when they pursue them in the labour market. However, tackling racism in schools remains an important task. Through the Race Relations Amendment Act, many of the systems are in place, but they are not implemented consistently enough. More serious attempts could be made to enforce already existing legal requirements on schools (Gilborn, 2004). At a time when schools are shifting towards a model of self-evaluation more generally and the introduction of new external accountability mechanisms may be regarded as regressive, the question is whether self policing in this area will ever be effective.

Maintaining momentum through the labour market

While the impact of socio-economic inequalities can be diminished through early years intervention and, to a lesser extent, school education, a person's background and their social, economic and cultural capital still play a very important role when young people enter the labour market. Therefore, policies to reduce inequalities in the distribution of income and wealth may have more of an impact on individuals' life chances than any other type of intervention. For Esping-Andersen, Scandinavia's egalitarianism can be explained to a great extent by their unusually compressed wage distribution. So what does the evolution of income inequality in Britain tell us about the chances of bringing about a more equal society?

In their chapter, Alissa Goodman *et al.* show that the 1980s and 1990s have seen very different trends in terms of income inequality. In the 1980s, income differentials widened across the whole population, while relative poverty rates grew rapidly. The end of the 1990s have seen an unusual combination of slightly rising income inequality and falling relative poverty. This can be explained by the fact that overall levels of inequality have been driven by changes at the very top and the very bottom of the income distribution. For the eighty per cent of people who are in the middle range of this distribution, incomes have become a little bit more equal, with the incomes of the poorer ones rising slightly more than the richer ones.

Along with a recovering economy, an important factor behind the falling rates of relative poverty and the improved equality in the middle income range have been policies introduced by Labour since 1997, particularly the large increases in means-tested benefits and tax credits. However, even this relatively large redistributive programme has only been able to slow down the growth in inequality, but by no means to reduce it, which gives an indication of the efforts that will be needed to make further gains. Also, the benefits have been limited to groups that have been particularly targeted by the government: families with children and pensioners. The distribution of income after tax credits and benefits are taken into account shows that poverty among childless couples and single people has grown to record levels.

Sue Harkness's analysis of gender pay inequality adds further details to this general picture. The gender pay gap for full time workers has decreased significantly since 1990, particularly for the lowest paid and less well educated women thanks to an increase in the demand for their work in the service sector and the introduction of the national minimum wage. For women working part-time, however, relative pay has changed little over the last thirty years, at around sixty per cent of the average full-time hourly male wage. The pay penalty to having children has also been reduced since the end of the 1990s, thanks to policy reforms which have improved support for childcare and working parents and extended maternity leave. However, these benefits are less pronounced for those with more than one child and for mothers who work part-time. This suggests that there is still some way to go, even for those groups that have received specific attention in recent years.

Redistribution through tax credits and benefits has put the government on course to meet its target of cutting the number of children brought up in poverty by one-quarter between 1998–9 and 2004–5. However, achieving the government's target of halving child poverty by 2010 through tax and benefit policies will require further enormous efforts.

In his paper, Mike Brewer shows that it might require up to two billion pounds a year by 2007–8 to fund more generous tax credits and means-tested benefits to maintain progress towards the target. However, this would be at the cost of reducing financial work incentives for parents. If work incentives are to be maintained, the costs to the exchequer will be even higher. Other, necessarily expensive, policies focusing on young children's health, care and education, such as have been highlighted above, might have a deeper and longer-term impact on reducing child poverty in the very long run. But how can the government afford to pay for these policies while simultaneously transferring resources to today's families to meet the child poverty target in the medium term?

At the other end of the spectrum, the top one per cent of people with the highest incomes have seen them increase sharply throughout the 1980s and 1990s. Does this matter? To what extent should we worry about an increase in inequality that is not so much triggered by people falling further into poverty, but by high earners pulling further away? The pulling away of the top one per cent creates the danger of the very rich being able to use their wealth to influence the political process, for example through the funding of parties, as some observers believe happens in the US. But it also has a wider impact: if the top one per cent is perceived to be living by other rules, the legitimacy of the whole system might be called into question. While the reasons for this are not clear, Esping-Andersen argues that international comparisons also show that higher levels of income inequality are associated with lower levels of social mobility, which also suggests an important role for policies to reduce income inequality.

Labour came to power with a 'welfare to work' programme, where paid work for fair pay was seen as the main way of getting people out of poverty. While unemployment has fallen sharply since 1997, economic inactivity is still high.

In his chapter, Peter Robinson argues that Labour's employment policies have implied a necessary trade-off between the agenda of 'tackling inactivity' and that of 'promoting retention and progression'. In other words, the capacities of Jobcentre Plus have been devoted to getting people into work, rather than ensuring that they would then stay in their job and progress further in the labour market. This may have led to disappointing results on an individual basis, but can be seen as the most cost-efficient use of resources.

Jobcentre Plus is based on a 'job first' model, where the priority is to get people to work, hoping that this will give them experience, credentials and incentives that will improve their position in the labour market. According to Peter Robinson, this is the right choice, as opposed to a 'human capital' approach that would focus on providing more training to the unemployed. Most learning pays off, but not all qualifications get a good return. In this case, giving more choice to adult learners could be more beneficial than offering them an undifferentiated diet of level 2 NVQs, which bring little returns in terms of higher wages. However, if we see the government's political capital with employers as limited, training might not be the most important policy to focus on. As we have seen earlier, increasing parental leave could be more effective in reducing socio-economic inequalities and should therefore be prioritised.

The Jobcentre Plus model coupled with tax and benefit changes has managed to reduce unemployment among target groups (young people and lone parents in particular) at a relatively low cost. However, further significant gains are likely to be more difficult, as the focus shifts towards categories of people who are more difficult to reach, such as people with disabilities and those with no qualifications. The skills and competencies of Jobcentre Plus personal advisers are crucial in this regard. But they are not very well rewarded, with low pay, little training and a voluminous case load that allows for little contact time (Finn, 2004). We noted that workforce issues were essential in the early years. They are as important at this later stage of people's lives, when they are looking for assistance from well-qualified staff to help them secure a place in the labour market.

According to Paul Gregg (2004), wide pay inequalities within groups with similar qualifications suggest that they are not due solely to education. Other factors come into play when people are entering the labour market and then try to progress through it. Cognitive skills, literacy and numeracy, soft skills and personality traits such as communication and behaviour are all rewarded through an increase in the wages of those possessing them. Physical attributes, beauty for example, also have a correlation with wages which still needs to be explained. The worrying fact is that skills and traits again owe more to family background and the cultural capital accumulated through rubbing shoulders with a favourable social milieu. More research needs to be done on how traits acquired through family background are transmitted into education and later attainments. We then need to assess the potential for policies that not only try to reduce the role of social inheritance at the beginning of a life cycle, but that might reduce its impact later on.

The most common explanation used to explain the growth of wage inequality over the last decades has been technological change biased towards highly skilled workers. In parallel, globalisation is deemed to have created increased competition between firms and enabled some multi-national companies to transfer their operations to countries with cheaper labour. This, in turn, has led to a loss of low skilled jobs, mainly in the industrial sector. However, the labour market shows more of a polarisa-tion between the two ends of the spectrum, both of which are growing: the managerial, professional and technical jobs on one side and less paid, low skilled personal services and retail jobs, with the latter very often servicing those at the top. What we need to understand better is why continuing globalisation and liberalisation can have been associated with a massive increase in wage inequality in the 1980s, but a more modest increase in the 1990s, and with market income inequality showing little change in recent years.

Conclusion

Some common themes cropped up in many of the various sessions of the Forum. The most obvious starting point for any summation is to reflect on the areas where there seems most clearly to be the need for further research.

- It is still not clear how cost-effective interventions to support parenting are, in part because of the lack of systematic evaluation of so many small scale schemes.

- We need to think further about how best to maintain momentum through the years of compulsory schooling to build upon the gains that might be made in the early years. It is still not clear how we should allo-cate resources across the five to sixteen or indeed the nought to sixteen phase of learning to best effect.

- It remains a significant puzzle why market income inequality in the UK has not been rising further in recent years when such economic drivers as technological change and 'globalisation' have not obviously abated.

- We would like to know more about the top one per cent of the income distribution as well as addressing the question of whether or not we should care about them.

- We need urgently to learn more about what combination of policy instruments can best tackle economic inactivity amongst disadvantaged adults and help promote retention and progression for those at the lower end of the labour market.

- We need to know more about the returns to skills in the labour market, about which we know relatively little, as opposed to qualifications, about which we know quite a lot.

Issues relating to the public service workforce were common to many of the presentations and were reflected in many of the discussions. Though they are unlikely to recognise it, the schools' workforce is relatively well-off compared to their colleagues at either end of the learning system, with both the early years workforce and the workforce in further education being on average less-well qualified and less well-paid, despite the importance of their role in providing early chances and second chances. There are widespread concerns about whether critical adult services like Jobcentre Plus have the staffing resources necessary to fulfil their ambitious agendas.

The question of how different public agencies can best join-up their activities will always be a recurring theme in public policy. Bringing together the disparate range of local children's services under the remit of the new Children's Trusts will be a major challenge; ensuring the effective coordination of those trusts with other key agencies including Primary Care Trusts and Jobcentre Plus will be at least as challenging. Clarifying the responsibilities of 'autonomous' public agencies such as schools to the wider community is another conundrum, partly of policy makers' own creation.

All the presentations and discussions highlighted the key theme of how to marry an ambitious policy agenda with limited resources. British policy makers would like to develop universal early years provision on a par with Scandinavia. We would like a well-resourced and staffed schools system to build on the gains made in the early years and further and higher education and training that gives all a chance to progress further. We want to help the economically inactive back into employment and we want to offer the low paid chances for progression. We want to continue to reduce child poverty in the medium term and to create the conditions to eliminate it in the long term. All these ambitions require resources and the popular support necessary to see them through. What is not yet clear is how we address what seems the central paradox of this agenda, that of the UK apparently wanting a Scandinavian welfare state but with Anglo-Saxon levels of taxation.

References

Edwards, L. (2004) 'Parenting for equal life chances' Presentation at the Social Mobility and Life Chances Forum – Maintaining Momentum, 3–4.12.04

Finn, D. (2004) 'Inactivity' Presentation at the Social Mobility and Life Chances Forum – Maintaining Momentum, 3–4.12.04

Gilborn, D. (2004) 'Maintaining momentum through race equality in schools' Presentation at the Social Mobility and Life Chances Forum – Maintaining Momentum, 3–4.12.04

Glass, N. (2005) 'Surely some mistake?', *Society Guardian*, 05.1.05

Gregg, P. (2004) 'Pay inequality', Presentation at the Social Mobility and Life Chances Forum – Maintaining Momentum, 3–4.12.04

Moss, P. (2004) 'Early Years: Building from an emerging consensus?' Presentation at the Social Mobility and Life Chances Forum – Maintaining Momentum, 3–4.12.04

Sammons, P., Sylva K. (2004) 'Maintaining momentum in primary schools' Presentation at the Social Mobility and Life Chances Forum – Maintaining Momentum, 3–4.12.04

Schuemer, G. (2004) 'What can we learn from international comparisons – PISA disentangled' Presentation at the Social Mobility and Life Chances Forum – Maintaining Momentum, 3–4.12.04

Steer, A. (2004) 'Maintaining momentum through curriculum reform' Presentation at the Social Mobility and Life Chances Forum – Maintaining Momentum, 3–4.12.04

2 Social inheritance and equal opportunity policies
Gosta Esping-Andersen

In a world of genuine equal opportunity our life chances would largely depend on effort, motivation, and skills and very little on the luck of birth. For very good reasons, social scientists over the past half century were confident that social inheritance of life chances, or ascription, would wane. For one, the democratisation of education should eliminate perhaps the most iportant filter of traditional class privilege, namely parents' unequal ability to invest in their children's human capital. For another, as postindustrial theorists like Daniel Bell (1976) insist, the knowledge intensive economy will prioritise merit and ability over ascriptive characteristics. And, thirdly, since economic want and insecurity in families have adverse effects on schooling, the expansion of the welfare state ought to have contributed decisively in leveling the playing field.

We confront, therefore, a major puzzle because a cumulation of social scientific evidence suggests that individuals' life chances remain as powerfully determined by their social origins as in the epoch of our fathers and grandfathers. This is cause for worry if we care about social justice, and also quite problematic if we are concerned with our future economy. The evolving knowledge economy will 'up the ante' in terms of the skills and qualifications necessary for a good life. Those who acquire insufficient human capital today will, with growing likelihood, find themselves locked into a life of low pay and precariousness. And, if a large share of today's youth fails to realise its full productive potential, tomorrow's retirees will be less well off.

This chapter opens with a review of what we know about social inheritance and life chances, focusing especially on the key mechanisms that perpetuate unequal opportunities. The bad news is that social inheritance has not, in any meaningful way, abated. But there is some good news because recent research has uncovered a few non-trivial exceptions to the rule. If we can identify the precise mechanisms at work, this might help us redefine the pursuit of more equality of opportunity. The last part of the chapter is therefore devoted to an assessment of policy alternatives. To anticipate my conclusions, I am sceptical about the standard assumption that generational inheritance is driven primarily by unequal investments in education. Instead, the decisive mechanisms probably concentrate in conditions prior to children's first encounter with the class room. It is in early childhood that parental transmission is key. Poverty and economic insecurity are very problematic but the 'cultural capital' of families is arguably decisive. This would indicate that research and public policy need to change the focus from education systems towards families and early childhood welfare.

Recent evidence on social inheritance

In a rare example of disciplinary convergence, sociologists and economists study inter-generational inheritance (or mobility) pretty much the same way and produce similar conclusions. The only real difference is that economists focus on earnings and incomes, while sociologists mainly examine educational, occupational, or social class attainment.[1] In reality the difference of focus matters little since the main mobility variables – income or occupational destiny – are pretty much two sides of the same coin. Earnings and occupational status are, unsurprisingly, highly correlated (Erikson and Goldthorpe, 1992), as are earning and class (Wright, 1979).[2]

Both disciplines also assume a similar causal logic. Both agree that education is the crucial site where social inheritance is transmitted. Human capital theory, as developed by Becker (1964), and more recently by Becker and Tomes (1979; 1986), argues that offsprings' income correlates highly with parental income because parents are unequally able to invest in their children's education. It is therefore not surprising that social scientists believed so readily that opportunities would become more equal. The impact of parental investments should logically diminish if access to education is democratised and if government investment in education is to the greatest benefit of lower income families. In most advanced countries, postwar education reforms were designed to accomplish precisely that. Hence the emphasis on comprehensive school systems, late (if any) streaming, scholarships, and bridges between the branches of the educational system.

Early US research on inter-generational income mobility produced fairly optimistic results. Parent-child correlations were found to hover around 0.2 to 0.3, and this suggested a fairly modest degree of social inheritance (Solon, 1999). These studies, however, were riddled with methodological problems and recent, more robust, estimates now converge around a far higher core figure (of about 0.4) for the United States. There is credible support for the prediction that changes in income distribution and/or in government investment in education will affect the elasticity. Harding *et al.* (2002) demonstrate a continuous decline in the US correlation that is related both to government expenditure and to declining household income dispersion during the 1960s and 1970s. Interestingly, rising inequalities thereafter have produced a reversal.

Comparisons with other countries are, of course, better suited to test the effects of differing educational policies. In one of the early studies of income mobility between generations, Atkinson *et al.* (1983) showed very strong parent-child correlations for Britain. More recent research pretty much confirms this picture (Solon, 1999; Corak, 2004). Indeed, Blanden *et al.* (2004) show that government policy may actually reinforce – rather than weaken – the social origins effect if, as in Britain, the expansion of higher education has mainly been to the benefit of the privileged classes.

1 But this distinction is far from perfect. Sociologists such as Robert Hauser and Christopher Jencks have studied earnings determination intensively; economists, such as Freeman, and Bowles and Gintis have studied educational attainment.

2 For general overviews, see Featherman and Hauser (1976), Erikson and Goldthorpe (1992), Hauser and Warren (1997), and Sorensen (2001).

Within the comparative literature, the US, followed by Britain, emerge as substantially less mobile than other countries. Bjorklund and Jantti (1997) compare Sweden and the US and find substantially greater inter-generational income mobility in the former (a correlation around 0.2). Estimates for Germany also suggest more mobility than in the US or Britain (Corak, 2004). Comparatively speaking, the Nordic countries (Denmark and Sweden) exhibit systematically more intergenerational income mobil-ity while the UK and US (and Italy) fall at the other extreme (Jorgensen, 2001).

That the US is far less mobile than Germany and Sweden may come as a surprise considering the unregulated nature of its labour markets and the prevailing mobility myth. It also contradicts one of the main theoretical premises of sociological research, namely the thesis that modernisation, i.e. economic growth and industrialisation, will, in the long run, increase mobility opportunities – and thus undo the class divide.[3] It was assumed, rather than demonstrated, that the United States – as the vanguard of economic development – boasted substantially more social fluidity than elsewhere. And it was predicted that Europe, and even Third World nations, would eventually exhibit similarly high mobility rates once the economic catch-up process caught on.[4] Clearly, the comparative research on intergen-erational income mobility has given this thesis the death-knell.

Turning to sociological research, the new consensus, as far as long-run historical evolution is concerned is best captured by Erikson and Goldthorpe's notion of the 'constant fl,ux'. That is, the correlation between social origins and achievement appears extraordinarily stable and trend-less over long historical periods in just about all societies.[5] And this holds for occupational class mobility (Erikson and Goldthorpe, 1992), and for educational attainment (Shavit and Blossfeld, 1993). Yet, these very same studies do identify exceptions to the constant flux, particularly among the youngest cohorts in Sweden, and arguably also in the Netherlands. Subsequent analyses corroborate this (Erikson and Jonsson, 1996). In brief, just as the economists find exceptionally low intergenerational correlations in Sweden, so the sociologists identify Sweden as a unique case of dimin-ishing social inheritance.

Virtually all intergenerational mobility research shows strong assym-etries across social classes or income groups. Atkinson et al. (1983) found that there was far more immobility at the very top and at the bottom of the social hierarchy: most of the mobility that does occur is concentrated in the middle. Ermisch and Francesconi (2004) suggest that, in Britain, downward mobility from the top of the class structure is far less likely than is upward mobility from the bottom. A Danish study illustrates the logic well. Denmark is also in the vanguard in terms of income mobility. Indeed, within the second, third and fourth quintiles there is virtually no correla-tion between parents' and children's incomes. In other words, virtually the

3 A subse-quent revision of the thesis argued that rising mobil-ity would mainly occur in the initial stages of industri-alisation, after which mobility flows would stabilise (Featherman, Jones and Hauser, 1975). For an overview, see Grusky and Hauser (1984).

4 In practice the mod-ernisation hypothesis that guided sociologi-cal mobility research has a close kin-ship to the thesis in economics that earn-ings begin to regress to the mean as countries become rich (Solon, 1999:1779).

5 It is impor-tant to note here that we are referring to net mobil-ity rates, i.e. net of changes in the marginals of parent-child mobility matrices.

entire social inheritance effect for Denmark is concentrated within the two extremes (Jorgensen, 2001: Table II.17). But the mobility disadvantage that the poorest face (and the advantage that the richest enjoy) in Denmark is far less than in other countries. The core problem of social inheritance lies buried in the extremes. Children of the poor face exceptionally tough barriers to move up in the hierarchy; children of the rich appear unusually protected. The challenge is to understand the mechanisms at work.

Sociologists have always been preoccupied with the mechanisms that connect origins and destinations, especially with those that may jointly explain both educational and job inheritance. Most sociologists will interpret inter-generational mobility correlations in terms of two main kinds of social interactions: firstly, the social milieu of the family during childhood and youth (such as family stability, poverty, or 'cultural capital') and, secondly, the characteristics of the social community (neighbourhood class or race segregation, or social networks).[6]

The mechanisms of inter-generational transmission

In the postwar era there has been an almost perfect consensus that education is the chief mechanism through which origins are linked to destinations. Reformers put their faith in educational reform, but their faith was largely misplaced, and this requires explanation.

We can look at the effect of education at a micro or macro level. In the former case, the system is a given and research focuses on the processes of social selection within that system. In the latter, as in cross-national mobility comparisons, research focuses on educational systems, with whether one model promotes more or less opportunity than an another.

Many of those studies that compare across systems present puzzling nation-differences. For example, Shavit and Blossfeld (1993) find that Sweden, alone among a large number of countries, has managed to rupture the constant flux.[7] Swedish (and Danish) public expenditure on education does lie a couple of percentage points above the OECD mean. But comparative educational attainment research, as well as international evaluation studies, suggest that differences in public educational spending matter very little (Shavit and Blossfeld, 1993; Eriksson and Jonsson, 1996; OECD, 2001).

System design might conceivably be of greater importance. It is, for example, an established fact that early streaming in schools reinforces social inequalities. And the Swedish reform of its comprehensive school system was explicitly designed to augment equal opportunities. But Denmark never embarked on comprehensiveness. Educational system characteristics (such as tracking, or the mix of public and private schools) may help account for group-specific mobility patterns, but they generally fail to explain overall mobility differences. Hence, the constant flux of occupational or educational attainment prevails in countries with distinctly dif-

6 Economists like Borjas (1995) and Corcoran et.al. (1992) have begun to move in similar directions. In this chapter I will not address the community effects, mainly because they are empirically less salient than the family effects.

7 Their study did not include any of the other Scandinavian countries.

8 The main
results from
OECD's (2001)
PISA study
corroborate
this. It shows
that variations
in youth (aged
about fifteen)
educational
and cognitive
performance
are predomi-
nantly related
to family-of-
origin varia-
bles. National
differences in
school sys-
tems, or even
intra-national
variations in
the quality of
teachers and
schools, make
little differ-
ence.

9 Erikson
and Jonsson
(1996) suggest
the possibil-
ity that the
comprehen-
sive Swedish
system may
have helped
create more
educational
equality. Yet,
they remain
quite sceptical
as to whether
this is what
accounts for
the declin-
ing social
inheritance
effects found
for Sweden.
In fact, also
Denmark
and Norway
(previously
un-studied)
exhibit a
similar (and
very strong)
declining
inheritance
effect, and
their educa-
tion systems

ferent educational systems – such as the United States, Germany, Italy and the UK, four countries that pretty much represent the global diversity in education systems.[8] Nor is it easy to explain the two deviant cases by refer-ence to system attributes. Danish education is quite similar to the German dual system while Sweden (since the 1960s) boasts a comprehensive school system that, in many respects, recalls the American – although it is far less heterogeneous in terms of quality and financing.[9]

When we move to micro-analyses, the education variable comes closer to the individualised investment-logic that drives economic theory. But if we doubt that it is all money-driven, we need to broaden our search for the smoking gun. In fact, since education hardly ever explains more than a fifth of the variation in log-earnings (Card, 1999), the gun is bound to be located elsewhere.

Sociologists generally prefer to study educational attainment in terms of transitions rather than years of education (Mare, 1993). This is so for two principal reasons. One, the social origins effect is not monotonic by years of schooling. It is stronger at earlier key transitions (in particular transi-tions into secondary education) and tapers off later on. Put differently, if 'poor' kids make it through the hurdles, their performance is more on par with 'rich' kids. There is, in other words, a potential problem of selection bias when we measure education simply in terms of years of schooling.[10] Two, the important selection occurs at the moment youth face transitions, because it is at this point that they (and their parents) will calculate the potential gains, risks, and opportunity costs associated with additional schooling (Breen, 2001). The risk calculus is, itself, likely to co-vary with the mechanisms (such as income, social networks or cultural capital) that link social origins to educational outcomes. What, then, determines educational choices and outcomes?

An important clue comes from research on remedial education (Heckman, 1999). One solid finding is that attempts to correct for skill-deficiencies later in life are ineffective if people do not already possess adequate motivational or cognitive resources to begin with. This, as devel-opmental psychologists have established, all begins in early childhood, in particular in the ages nought to six, which is when the basic abilities for learning are most intensely developed (Danziger and Waldfogel, 2000; Duncan and Brooks-Gunn, 1997).[11] This said, one would expect that family effects will overshadow community or neighbourhood effects (which are more likely to assert their influence at later stages).[12]

There is now consistent evidence that the family milieu during early childhood is decisive for later achievement, and also for later social prob-lems, such as school drop-out and criminality. One factor that has been studied extensively is the impact of poverty and, more generally, of family resources (Duncan, 1998; Duncan and Brooks-Gunn, 1997; Machin, 1998; McCulloch and Joshi, 2002). Indeed, the effects can be very powerful, as illustrated by American estimates that show that poverty in childhood is associated with an average of two years less of schooling and substantially lower earnings as adult (Mayer, 1997; Duncan, 1998). There is also strong evidence that family instability, unemployment, and alcoholism seriously impair children's educational attainment. Additionally, there is some evidence that mothers' employment may be harmful for children's development, but this is a disputed issue (Ermisch and Francesconi, 2002; Duncan and Brooks-Gunn, 1997).

Since many of these family characteristics, like unemployment, are correlated with parental income it is not easy to disentangle the real mechanisms. Financial security within the family no doubt plays a key role for how parents and their children make decisions at the moment of educational transitions. The perceived risks associated with continuing education are likely to be more intense in families that feel financially insecure. But other characteristics are not necessarily correlated with income. Inspired by Bourdieu's (1983) notion of 'cultural capital', there is a growing literature which suggests that social skills, personality traits, and cultural capital may be as important as educational certificates in career progression (Jencks *et al.*, 1979; DiMaggio, 1982; DiMaggio and Mohr, 1985; de Graaf *et al.*, 1998; for an overview, see also Bowles *et al.*, 2001); and also that the cultural and educational resources of parents are vital for children's cognitive development and school performance (OECD, 2001). Cultural resources may also be decisive in allowing parents to better 'navigate' the educational system in the best interests of their offspring (Erikson and Jonsson, 1996).

That cognitive skills compete with education in dictating life chances is fairly well established. What comes as a surprise is that the two are only weakly correlated – in other words they capture different dimensions of human capital.[13] There is evidence that cognitive abilities, independently of educational attainment, affect life chances. Bowles *et al.*'s (2001: 1154) review of the econometric evidence from twenty-four studies concludes that 'a standard deviation difference in cognitive performance is associated with something less than a ten per cent increase in wages, and is in this respect roughly equivalent to a year of schooling'. Warren *et al.* (2002) show that formal educational qualifications matter in the early career stage (and then decline in importance) while cognitive skills assert a persistent effect throughout the career. Green and Riddell (2000) and Esping-Andersen (2004) find that cognitive abilities account for about a third of the 'returns to education' in earnings equations. There is strong support for the possibility that a good part of the inter-generational class inheritance effects we observe is mediated via parents' impact on children's cognitive development.

If that is so, we obviously need to examine a broader menu of parental characteristics, and we also need to focus more on what happens before children even start school. Some recent work has deepened the family context considerably by including direct information on cultural assets, such

are not of the comprehensive type. Echoing the growing consensus in the literature, we must probably look elsewhere for explanations.

10 Considering that early transitions, such as between elementary and lower secondary education, are near-universal, there is a good case to be made for a quadratic specification if years of education is used.

11 The decisiveness of early childhood is also highlighted in Jencks and Phillips' (1998) analysis of the black-white score gap.

12 Solon et al.'s (2000) attempt to distinguish the impact of neighbourhood from family effects show clearly that the latter are, by far, the most important (5:1).

13 Using IALS data, the simple bi-variate correlation hovers between 0.4 and 0.5, depending on country

as literature, reading, and cultural consumption (de Graaf, 1998; OECD, 2001; Esping-Andersen, 2004).

To the extent that cognitive abilities and education measure distinct attributes, and to the extent that the former are importantly determined in pre-school ages, we are in a position to account for the 'constant flux' of educational attainment. The selection mechanisms that occur in school systems are, in large part, already prefigured in that cognitively and motivationally strong children will profit far more from any given curriculum and teaching than will their weaker counterparts, regardless of what kind of school system prevails or of how well-financed it is.[14] In other words, if we want to identify the smoking gun behind the constant flux, parental influence on cognitive development may be a good place to start.

In previous work I have estimated, for eight countries, the impact of social origins (using parents' education and socioeconomic status as measures) on their childrens' educational attainment and cognitive performance. In these kinds of estimations it is vital that we control for gender and especially for immigrant status. Girls normally perform better than boys and non-natives are at a disadvantage in terms of administered cognitive tests. A summary of the results is presented in Table 2.1.

Table 2.1 The impact of social origins on educational attainment and on cognitive performance in eight countries (ages 30-40)

| | coefficients for | | | |
| | child's years of education[1] | | child's cognitive score | |
	β	standard beta	β	standard beta
Canada	.080	.423	5.055	.411
US	.206	.424	10.251	.364
UK	.489	.331	11.247	.284
Sweden	.085	.339	6.203	.338
Norway	.105	.328	6.064	.286
Denmark	.277	.259	4.397	.204
Germany	.803	.403	4.051	.105
Netherlands	.319	.377	4.987	.251

Note: All estimates are significant at .001 or better. The cognitive performance variable is the mean individual score on the three literacy items tested in the IALS (document, prose, and quantitative abilities). Note also that the age bracket for Canada is 25-35. All estimates include controls for gender and immigrant status.

1 β is adjusted for the differing variance in fathers' and children's education, i.e. $\beta = \beta(\sigma^2_y/\sigma^2_x)$

Source: IALS microdata (second wave)

14 This, in fact, is also the main conclusion from OECD's (2001) PISA study, which includes detailed information on children's cognitive performance, knowledge, and social background as well as on the schools and on 'neighbourhood effects'.

There are stark differences across countries in how much social origin influences schooling and cognitive skills. At one end we find (as usual) the UK and the US, with Canada, where the parental impact is unusually strong, especially with regard to children's cognitive performance. At the other end we find the three Scandinavian countries where, uniformly, parents' social status has a far more modest impact on their children's fate. To illustrate, the impact of parents' status is almost twice as strong in the US as it is in Denmark.

The analyses above focused on a single cohort (in their thirties). If we look at educational attainment for distinct cohorts we can identify whether there is any trend towards a weakening of the social inheritance effect. This amounts to a replication – and update – of the Shavit and Blossfeld (1993) studies. The great advantage of the International Adult Literacy Survey (IALS) data is that they include also the youngest generations born in the 1970s. It is this generation that, far more than any preceding one, will have drawn the benefits, if any, from postwar welfare state policies. As shown in Esping-Andersen (2004), most countries conform to the prevailing 'constant flux' consensus. If we begin with the oldest cohorts, born around 1940, we find a uniform and strong impact of parents' education on children's attainment. Across all countries children of parents with upper secondary level education are roughly two and a half times as likely to also attain the same level as those whose parents did not. As we move to the youngest cohorts, convergence turns to a sharp divergence. In one group of countries – the US, the UK, Germany, and Italy – the parental impact remains unchanged. But in the Nordic countries – and now Denmark is in the vanguard – the parental effect begins to weaken with the cohorts born in the 1960s and even more so with those born in the 1970s.

Since social inheritance is especially strong at the top and bottom of the social hierarchy it would be especially illuminating to focus on children of less educated parents, i.e. those with only primary level or less. Indeed, when we look at children from this social background, the uniqueness of the Nordic countries is even more accentuated. In line with our earlier results, the 'constant flux' best describes most countries but, led again by Denmark, the children of less educated parents in Scandinavia do continue to have a disadvantage but this disadvantage has been sharply reduced for the cohorts born since the 1960s. The odds that UK children of such parents will make it through upper secondary level is 2:10 compared to children of parents with secondary education. In Denmark, the odds are 5:10.[15]

However, this data does not help us to disentangle the precise mechanisms at work. Do children of higher status parents do better because parents invest more in their education, or is it the result of cultural transmission? The recently released PISA data, examining the cognitive abilities of fifteen to sixteen year olds in a large number of countries, permit a far more detailed seperation of income and culture factors.[16] The study does not include information on parental income, but does include a 'wealth' variable based on a composite of information on the size, standards, and

15 In this case, the UK performs rather better than the US and Germany (where the odds are only 1:10)

16 For a description of the PISA study, see OECD (2001).

quality of the parental home – arguably a reasonable proxy for income. It also includes an indicator score variable, weighting parents' occupation and income, information on father's and mother's education and employment status, and a range of variables that indicate the family's cultural milieu.

In the above-mentioned study I attempt to estimate the relative importance of culture versus money (Esping-Andersen, 2004). The analyses also address the debate on whether mothers' employment may have adverse consequences for children's cognitive development. The results point systematically to 'culture' as being the smoking gun we are looking for.

It is, first of all, evident in all countries studied that children's cognitive performance is far more powerfully related to the family's cultural capital than to income variables. The cultural capital variable (a composite measure of the quantity of books in the home, of frequency of discussing cultural themes, and of frequenting cultural events) explains roughly twice as much of the variation in cognitive abilities as do the income variables. Interestingly, the correlation between family income and family culture is quite low.

The impact of mothers' employment is, as noted, a controversial issue. In a study using British data, Ermisch and Francesconi (2002) conclude that the effect can be quite damaging. American research comes to more ambiguous findings and suggests, tentatively, that adverse effects – if any – are mainly acute when mothers work full-time and especially when their job is stressful (Duncan and Brooks-Gunn, 1996). What emerges from my analyses of the PISA data is that part-time employment is nowhere problematic and in a few countries, basically the Nordic, neither is full-time work. But, and this is worth noting, the impact is opposite for boys and girls. Indeed, for girls the effect is generally positive while for boys it is largely negative. Again, this gender-specific pattern is far less accentuated in Scandinavia than elsewhere.

If we now try to pull the evidence together, two sets of conclusions emerge. One, the transmission mechanisms are fairly similar across all countries. Family income matters but, if anything, it would appear that parental cultural capital is rather more decisive – at least as far as cognitive development and school success are concerned. Still, when we add that cognitive skills explain a substantial proportion of earnings variations, the effect is most likely present throughout the life course. Basically, as Mayer (1997) argues, money alone cannot buy equal opportunities.

All this would invite profound pessimism among reformers bent on creating a world of equal opportunities. While it is easy to forge policies to reform education systems it seems difficult to imagine how government can equalise families' cultural capital, let alone influence parents' cognitive stimulus. The national comparisons, however, suggest that the world is not necessarily preordained to a perpetual constant flux. There are three countries that systematically deviate: Denmark, Norway and Sweden. Inter-generational income mobility is far greater, occupational destinies and educational attainment are substantially less determined by the luck of birth and, most interestingly, cognitive abilities depend less on parental background. To this we might add that inequalities of cognitive abilities are markedly smaller than elsewhere. If we compute a Gini coefficient for cognitive test scores, the Danish coefficient is exactly half the American. The US and UK may not exactly deviate in the other direction, but they do stand out as being quite immobile in terms of life chances.

We are then left with the one overriding puzzle: why is the social inheritance of life chances so much weaker in Scandinavia than elsewhere? And why, starting from basically the same initial level, has it declined so significantly over the past twenty years?

Public policy and equality of opportunity

Since it would be difficult to explain Scandinavia's egalitarianism in terms of public investment in education, an alternative economic explanation might lie in their unusually compressed wage distributions which, de facto, implies that earnings are only weakly linked to human capital or gender. The US has one of the OECD's most unequal wage distributions, and hence one would expect that skill or other worker attributes play a far greater role in dictating individual incomes. No doubt there is some truth to this. Yet it fails to explain the fact that Scandinavia is also more egalitarian in terms of educational attainment, occupational mobility, and cognitive development.

It is very tempting, in fact, to explain it all tautologically: very inegalitarian societies beget very inegalitarian results. But the tautology disappears when we add to this that very inegalitarian societies also beget more ascription and less mobility.[17] This pattern emerges clearly in a comparison of national Gini coefficients and inter-generational income mobility (Table 2.2).

Table 2.2 Income inequality and social inheritance (countries ranked by Gini)

	Social mobility	Gini coefficient
Denmark	0.81	.22
Sweden	0.85	.23
Germany	0.75	.28
UK	0.71	.31
US	0.71	.34
Italy	0.67	.35

Source: Jorgensen (2001: Table II.18)

Note: social mobility refers to the association between parental and child income. A coefficient of 1.00 would denote perfect mobility and the lower the number, the less mobility.

17 Corak (2001) has also argued that inter-generational correlations will be higher in more unequal societies, and his study also stresses the centrality of non-monetary factors, such as parents' cultural stimulation.

This quite astounding covariation runs counter to the prevailing thesis that income inequality stimulates incentives for mobility. In fact, all the data we have examined suggest that mobility is negatively related to levels of overall inequality. The causal direction is unclear. It may be that pervasive social inheritance predestines a society to be more unequal on all dimensions of distribution. It may also be that causality goes in the opposite direction: if income inequalities are huge the poor will have to travel a greater distance to reach the middle. For policy making it would be futile to speculate on which is the real chicken and egg because if inequality and mobility co-vary, an effective policy intervention in one or the other would have effects on both. The great policy challenge is to identify the crucial point that will untie the Gordian Knot.

One important conclusion is that we must abandon our faith in education policy as the great leveller because the inequalities are to a great extent established prior to school age. Of course, education systems can contribute to strengthening or weakening these and as the OECD's (2001) review of the evidence makes clear, any overall strategy for equal opportunities must also include attributes of the school system – in particular avoiding early tracking, class or ethnic segmentation, favouring comprehensive schools, and promoting bridges between educational branches. In brief, the main egalitarian aim of education policy is probably to see that schools do not simply reproduce or even worsen the inequalities that already have been created.

The second important conclusion is that 'money' may be important but that it is not a sufficient precondition for good life chances. We know that economic hardship in childhood has potentially very negative effects on educational attainment and later life chances. How precisely it works is not fully evident but it is safe to say that the impact is pervasive throughout childhood and probably most acute at moments of transition from compulsory to non-compulsory levels. Income-poor families are less resourceful, less able to plan ahead and 'navigate the school system', and poor parents are more likely to spur their children to abandon school in favour of a job. A policy of guaranteeing against child poverty would no doubt be very effective and, as it turns out, it is financially cheap. If we were to peg the guarantee to fifty per cent of median income, the additional public outlay would not exceed 0.2 per cent of GDP in most countries (Esping-Andersen and Sarasa, 2002).[18]

When we more closely examine why there is so little child poverty in Scandinavia it turns out that public income transfers are far less important than the mere fact that just about all mothers are employed. Child poverty in two income families is everywhere modest and declines precipitously among employed lone mothers, too. Swedish lone mothers boast an employment rate near eighty per cent and a poverty rate of only four per cent.

18 Our calculations suggest an additional expenditure of 0.22 per cent of GDP for the UK.

Encouraging mothers' employment necessitates affordable child care, which in Scandinavia is practically universal for the nought to six age bracket. There is no a priori reason for publicly provided child care if our sole aim is to facilitate women's employment. American mothers are also now typically employed and use daycare. But American daycare is almost exclusively privately provided and the quality of care will correlate strongly with parental income (Blau, 2001). American day care is of extremely uneven quality, and children from disadvantaged families are likely to find themselves concentrated at the low end. This contrasts with Scandinavian care which is basically of uniform, high standards, meaning that children from disadvantaged families will benefit disproportionately.

The upshot is that a policy designed for altogether different objectives, namely to reconcile work and motherhood, has the potential of equalising the stimulus structure for pre-school children. Indeed, the uneven distribution of cultural capital among families is greatly neutralised if, as in the Nordic countries, virtually all children from age one to six participate in a child care system that is of homogeneously high quality. As long as cognitive and motivational stimulus is predominantly internalised in the family, as is the case in almost all societies, the effect is to reproduce the cultural differentials of the parental generation. The market model, exemplified by the US, will also reproduce differentials, in this case due to uneven quality in care. The uniqueness of the Scandinavian model, at least in the last two to three decades is that a crucial part of pre-school stimulation is shifted from parents to centres *that do not replicate social class differences*.

Recent evaluation research concludes similarly. As Waldfogel's (2002) review of both American and European research shows, child care programs that are intensive, intervene early, and that promote high standards contribute very effectively to raise the cognitive performance of children from disadvantaged milieux. In turn, this helps children start and proceed on a much more equal footing once they enter formal education. Although we have little longitudinal research, what evidence there is suggests that early quality care continues to exert positive emotional and cognitive results throughout childhood (Waldfogel, 2002:539).

High quality and universal child care is, in tandem with low child poverty, likely to be a key explanatory factor behind Scandinavia's success in reducing social inheritance. It is difficult to prove conclusively but all the data point in this direction. Most importantly, the decline in social inheritance effects on educational attainment coincides almost perfectly with the period (1970s-80s) in which child care attendance became the norm. The fact that the inheritance effect begins to drop for the cohorts born in the 1960s and then drops even further for those born in the 1970s adds credence to the argument. It was not until the 1980s that Denmark and Sweden arrived at near-universal coverage.

Therefore a promising strategy for equal opportunities will require a broad-based approach that encompasses educational policy, income redistribution and, as its flagship, major investments in pre-school institutions. There exist, however, several important caveats that may raise doubts as to its feasibility and effectiveness.

The exchequer will undoubtedly be the first to protest, arguing with reason that the financial costs of universal, high quality care are prohibitive. The per child cost of the Danish system is roughly 10,000 euros per year. But one thing is the up-front expenditure, another the long-term financial dynamics. If mothers have access to day care their work interruptions will be far shorter and this translates into far superior lifelong earnings (and tax payments). Calculations based on the Danish system indicate that working mothers will actually reimburse the initial cost over their lifetime career. Price-Waterhouse has undertaken a similar study for Britain and arrives at the same conclusion.

A second serious caveat has to do with the potential behavioral consequences of generous income guarantees to child families. A basic income guarantee will almost certainly not affect the labour supply of high income mothers, but it is likely to encourage low educated, low paid mothers to stay at home. If this occurs the upshot may be social polarisation. As I have argued the core problem of social inheritance is concentrated at the top and bottom of the social hierarchy. Scandinavia is successful on the equal opportunity front probably because children of low educated parents come to enjoy middle class cognitive stimulus via day care. This will not come about if there are incentives for low educated mothers to stay home with the children.

And this brings me to the third caveat. A strong argument against the child care formula is that mothers' (and parents') employment intensity may have adverse effects on their children's well being and school performance. Even if mothers' work may be positive because it reduces poverty, this should be weighed against the loss of quality and intensity in the parent-child interaction. As my brief review of the evidence suggested there are no unambiguous answers to this question. Mothers' part-time employment appears generally to be unproblematic. The main problems tend to be associated with long and stressful workdays – and it would seem that it is mainly boys that suffer.

It is also clear that the impact of parental employment varies by the phase of childhood. Negative effects are most visible in the youngest ages, zero to five. In the first years the key issue has mainly to do with the child's emotional security and there is accordingly a clear case to be made in favour of adequate maternity and parental leave time. In any case, parental employment effects will interact strongly with the quality of external care, asserting themselves far more negatively if children are placed in poor quality care. And there is also evidence that the gender of the parent matters little. What matters is that one of the parents is present. In other words, here is additional ammunition in favour of parental leave schemes and flexible work schedules that encourage take-up among both fathers and mothers.

In any case, the issue is not whether we should encourage a return to traditional familialism because women's lifelong paid employment is becoming the norm everywhere. This we must take for granted and, as such, we inevitably must address the challenge of making motherhood and careers compatible. The day care formula, if pursued along the Scandinavian line of universal coverage and high standards, will both enhance welfare and maybe also efficiency on two fronts simultaneously. It will help women pursue careers just when our aging society needs their employment. It will equalise the life chances of children while benefitting our economy by producing a more homogeneously productive and capable future workforce.

References

Atkinson, A., Maynard, A. and Trinder, C. (1983) *Parents and Children: Incomes in two generations* London: Heineman

Becker, G. (1964) *Human Capital* New York: Columbia University Press

Becker, G. and Tomes, N. (1979) 'An equilibrium theory of the distribution of income and intergenerational mobility' *Journal of Political Economy* 87:1153-1189

Becker, G. and Tomes, N. (1986) 'Human capital and the rise and fall of families' *Journal of Labor Economics* 4:1-39

Bjorklund, A. and Jantti, M. (1997) 'Intergenerational income mobility in Sweden compared to the United States' *American Economic Review* 87:1009-1018

Blanden, J., Goodman, A., Gregg, P. and Machin, S. (forthcoming) 'Changes in Intergenerational mobility in Britain' in Corak, M. (ed.) *The Dynamics of Intergenerational Mobility* Cambridge: Cambridge University Press

Blau, D. (2001) *The Childcare Problem* New York: Russell Sage

Blau, P. and Duncan O.D. (1967) *The American Occupational Structure* New York: John Wiley

Borjas, G. (1995) 'Ethnicity, neighbourhoods, and human capital externalities' *American Economic Review* 85:365-390

Bourdieu, P. (1983) 'The forms of capital' in Richardson J. (ed) *Handbook of Theory and Research in the Sociology of Education* Westport, CT: Greenwood

Bowles, S., Gintis, H. and Osborne, M. (2001) 'The determinants of earnings: A behavioural approach' *Journal of Economic Literature* XXXIX:1137-1176

Breen, R. (2001) 'A rational choice model of educational inequality' Instituto Juan March Working Paper 166 (October)

Card, D. (1999) 'The causal effect of education on earnings' in Ashenfelter, O. and Card, D. (eds) *Handbook of Labor Economics* 3 New York: Elsevier

Corak, M. (2001) 'Are the kids all right? Intergenerational mobility and child well-being in Canada' Working Paper 171, Family and Labour Studies, Statistics Canada

Corak, M. (ed) (2004) *The Dynmaics of Intergenerational Income Mobility* Cambridge: Cambridge University Press

Corcoran, M., Gordon, R., Laren, D. and Solon, G. (1992) 'The association between men's economic status and their family and community origins' *Journal of Human Resources* 27:575-601

Currie, J. (2001) 'Early childhood intervention programs' *Journal of Economic Perspectives* 15:213-238

Danziger, S. and Waldfogel, J. (2000) *Securing the Future: Investing in children from birth to college* New York: Russell Sage

DeGraaf, P. (1998) 'Parents' financial and cultural resources, grades, and transitions to secondary school' *European Sociological Review* 4:209-21

DiMaggio, P. (1982) 'Cultural capital and school success' *American Sociological Review* 47:189-201

DiMaggio, P. and Mohr, J. (1985) 'Cultural capital, educational attainment and marital selection' *American Journal of Sociology* 90:1231-61

Duncan, G. and Brooks-Gunn, J. (1997) *Consequences of Growing up Poor* New York: Russell Sage Foundation

Duncan, G. *et al.* (1998) 'The effects of childhood poverty on the life chances of children' *American Sociological Review* 63:406-23

Erikson, R. and Goldthorpe, J. (1992) *The Constant Flux* Oxford: Clarendon Press.

Erikson, R. and Jonsson, J. (1996) *Can Education be Equalised? The Swedish case in comparative perspective* Boulder, Col: Westview Press

Ermisch, J. and Francesconi, M. (2002) 'The effect of parents' employment on children's educational attainment' *ISER Working Paper* 21. University of Essex

Esping-Andersen, G. (2004) 'Untying the Gordian knot of social inheritance' *Research in Social Stratification and Mobility* 21:115-139

Esping-Andersen, G. and Sarasa, S. (2002) 'The generational conflict revisited' *Journal of European Social Policy* 12:5-22

Featherman, D. and Hauser, R. (1976) 'Prestige or socio-economic scales in the study of occupational achievement' *Sociological Methods and Research*

Featherman, D., Jones, F. and Hauser, R. (1975) 'Assumptions of social mobility research in the United States: The case of occupational status' *Social Science Research* 4:329-360

Green, D.A. and Riddell, W.C. (2000) 'Literacy, Numeracy and Labour Market Outcomes in Canada' Unpublished paper, Department of Economics, University of British Columbia (May)

Grusky, D. and Hauser, R. (1984) 'Comparative social mobility revisited' *American Sociological Review* 49:

Harding, D., Jencks, C., Lopoo, L. and Mayer, S. (2002) 'The changing effects of family background on the incomes of American adults' forthcoming in Bowles, S., Gintis, H. and Osborne M. (eds.) *Family Background and Economic Success* New York: Russell Sage

Haveman, R. and Wolfe, B. (1995) *Succeeding Generations: On the effects of investments in children* New York: Russell Sage Foundation

Heckman, J. (1999) 'Doing it right: job training and education' *The Public Interest* (Spring pp. 86-106)

Jencks, C., Smith, M., Acland, H., Bane M.J., Cohen, D., Gintis, H., Heyns, B. and Michelson, S. (1972) *Inequality: A reassessment of family and schooling in America* New York: Basic Books

Jencks, C. and Phillips, M. (1998) *The Black-White Test Score Gap* New York: Russell Sage

Jencks, C. and Phillips, M. (2001) 'Aptitude or achievement: why do test scores predict educational attainment and earnings?' in Mayer, S. and Peterson, P. (eds) *Cognitive and Social Skills: Sources, consequences and policy* Washington DC: Brookings Institute

Jorgensen, S. (2001) 'Analyser af indkomstfordelingen' Working Paper 2001:6 from Det Okonomiske Raad. Sekretariatet. Copenhagen.

Korpi, W. and Palme, J. (1998) 'The paradox of redistribution and strategies of equality' *American Sociological Review* 63:661-87

Machin, S. (1998) 'Childhood disadvantage and intergenerational transmissions of economic status' in Atkinson, A. and Hills, J. (eds) *Exclusion, Employment and Opportunity* London School of Economics (CASE)

Mare, R. (1993) 'Educational stratification and observed and unobserved components of family background' pp. 351-76 in Shavit, Y. and Blossfeld, H.P. (eds.) *Persistent Inequality* Boulder, Co: Westview Press

Mayer, S. (1997) *What Money Can't Buy* Cambridge, Mass: Harvard University Press

McCulloch, A. and Joshi, H. (2002) 'Child development and family resources: evidence from the second generation of the 1958 British birth cohort' *Journal of Population Economics* 15, 2:283-304

Mulligan, C. B. (1997) *Parental Priorities and Economic Inequality* Chicago: University of Chicago Press.

OECD (2000) *Literacy in the Knowledge Society* Paris: OECD

OECD (2001) *Education at a Glance* Paris: OECD

OECD (2001) *Knowledge and Skills for Life* Paris: OECD

Shavit, Y. and Blossfeld, H.P. (1993) *Persistent Inequality* Boulder: Col: Westview Press

Sieben, I., Huinink, J. and de Graaf, P. (2001) 'Family background and sibling resemblance in educational attainment' *European Sociological Review* 17, 4:401-430

Solon, G. (1992) 'Intergenerational income mobility in the United States' *American Economic Review* 82:393-408

Solon, G. (1999) 'Intergenerational Mobility in the Labor Market' pp. 1762-1800 in Ashenfelter, O. and Card, D. (eds.) *Handbook of Labor Economics* 3A.New York: Elsevier

Solon, G., Page, M. and Duncan, G. (2000) 'Correlations between neighbouring children in their subsequent educational attainment' *Review of Economics and Statistics* 82:383-92

Treiman, D. (1976) *Occupational Prestige in Comparative Perspective* New York: Academic Press

Waldfogel, J. (2002) 'Child care, women's employment, and child outcomes' *Journal of Population Economics* 15:527-48

Warren, J., Hauser, R. and Sheridan, J. 2002. 'Occupational stratification across the life course' *American Sociological Review* 67:432-55

Wright, E.O. (1979) *Class Structure and Income Determination* New York: Academic Press

Social mobility, life chances and the early years
Jane Waldfogel

Why the early years?

If the race is already halfway run even before children begin school, then we clearly need to examine what happens in the earliest years.

(Esping-Andersen, 2004)

Like it or not, the most important mental and behavioural patterns, once established, are difficult to change once children enter school.

(Heckman and Wax, 2004)

These statements summarise the two main reasons why the early years are a particularly important time for efforts to increase social mobility – a good deal of inequality is already apparent by the time children start school, and children's development may be less amenable to change once they enter school (see also Feinstein, 2003; Heckman and Lochner, 2000; Heckman and Masterov, 2004a; Phillips, Crouse, and Ralph, 1998). But, as compelling as these statements are, they do not tell us how much policies can reduce inequality in the early years, or what policies might be most effective.[1]

A host of studies, both in the US and the UK, have shown that there are multiple influences on development in the early years. These influences can be assigned to three main categories: child endowment; parents and the home environment; and preschool care and education.

So, although preschool care and education has been shown to effectively boost children's learning, not all the differences in children's attainment at school entry are due to differences in preschool care and education. Children start life with different endowments – of health, temperament, and so on. Some of these differences are due to genes, some to environmental effects (including differences in the pre-birth environment), and some to gene-environment interactions. A second important set of influences has to do with parents and the home environment (community environments may also play a role, but these effects are likely to operate indirectly through their influence on parents and the home environment). Children are affected by how much stimulation parents provide and how sensitive their care is. These aspects of parental care in turn are affected by income and financial hardship, the parents' own endowment with respect to health, ability, and so on, the parents' mental health, and the number of, and role played by, other family and household members (siblings, other adults, and so on).

1 I am grateful to colleagues at the Centre for Analysis of Social Exclusion (CASE) at the London School of Economics where I was a visitor during the 2003-4 academic year. I would also like to thank Paul Gregg and Katherine Magnuson for many helpful conversations, and Sakiko Tanaka for producing estimates from the Millennium Cohort Survey. An earlier version of this paper was presented at an IPPR/HM Treasury Conference on Social Mobility and Life Chances in April 2004 and at seminars at CASE and the Social Market Foundation in the summer of 2004.

Ideally, we would like to know from research how much each of these influences matter, and how amenable they are to policy intervention. But research is rarely able to precisely identify the exact share of variation due to different influences, and estimating policies' effects can be difficult as well. A general finding is that although both parental care and preschool care and education play a role in facilitating or hindering children's development in the early years, what parents do generally matters more than what preschools do. At the same time, however, another general finding is that interventions that provide high-quality care and education to children are more effective in changing outcomes, particularly in the cognitive domain, than interventions aimed at improving home environments and parental behaviour. Thus, although parenting may be more important, interventions to improve non-parental care and education may be more effective.

These considerations also suggest that when we think about policies to promote development in the early years, we need to think about how they affect each of these three sets of influences. Policies may moderate the effect of a child's endowment on development (by for example identifying and providing early treatment for a disability or health problem), may enable or encourage parents to provide a more nurturing and stimulating home environment (by reducing financial hardship or addressing mental health problems), or may improve the care and education the child receives outside the home (by moving children into care or education earlier, or for more hours, or by improving the quality of care and education they receive). The concept of multiple influences also means that we should not expect one type of intervention to address all the differences in children's attainment at school entry – multiple causes are likely to require multiple remedies. And, we may not yet have policy instruments to address all the sources of variation that exist.

What outcomes?

The focus of this paper is on what we know about how policies in the early years can promote more social mobility, breaking or at least mitigating the links that currently exist between the position of a child's family of origin and his or her eventual life position. However, stating that social mobility is the goal does not make clear what outcomes are of concern. Although often the most emphasis tends to be placed on cognitive development, ideally we would like to see more equality across all three of the main domains of child well-being: child health; child cognitive development; and child social and emotional development. Moreover, as a practical matter, we are coming to learn more about how problems of child health or social and emotional development may hinder disadvantaged children's school readiness and eventual school achievement (see Rouse, Brooks-Gunn, and McLanahan, forthcoming; Rothstein, 2003). Thus, even if we wish to prioritise policies that promote equality of school attainment, we should at least be aware of their potential effects on child health and child social and emotional development.

We also need to be aware of other priorities for policy-making. I highlight five, each of which is an important goal for public policy and directly or indirectly related to social mobility. First, promoting social inclusion (or reducing social exclusion) is an explicit goal of the current government and may also be key to promoting better outcomes for the disadvantaged (if for instance there are beneficial composition or peer effects of participating in programs with more advantaged children). Second, reducing child poverty is also an explicit goal of government and again may be key to promoting better outcomes through reducing financial hardship for parents and providing extra resources that could be devoted to child learning or development. Third, increasing parental employment in low-income families is another explicit goal of government and may also support better outcomes for disadvantaged children in various ways (boosting family income, promoting social inclusion, improving family routines, and so on) although it may also pose risks for some children (e.g. very young children placed in poor quality care for long hours). Then there are two wider objectives of public policy, not specific to this area but more cross-cutting – supporting parental choice, and promoting gender equity. These outcomes are relevant because they may be affected by early years policy, but also because they may themselves influence the effectiveness of policy. In the early years area, where the match between a caregiver or program and the needs of the individual child is key, choice becomes particularly important (see, for instance, Alakeson, 2004). Moreover, families who choose what program their child participates in may be more satisfied and may also be able to exert more influence over that program's quality, although parents may not always be counted on to choose a high-quality program. Gender clearly plays a role as well. Although we may talk about the role of parents, the bulk of the caregiving in the early years is done by mothers, and policies in the area of parental leave and child care and education can have a powerful impact on their position in the labour market, and in the home.

Keeping these other policy objectives in mind, social mobility, and in particular social mobility with regard to cognitive attainment, clearly merits special attention. The UK (like the US) has high levels of inequality, and high correlations between outcomes for parents and outcomes for their children (Blanden, Gregg, and Machin, 2003). For example, the Gini coefficient for quantitative literacy is 0.121 in the UK (and 0.133 in the US), vs 0.071 in Finland, 0.072 in Denmark, 0.081 in Sweden and Norway, 0.083 in Germany, and 0.097 in Italy (Esping-Anderson, 2004). Countries where fathers' educational attainment is highly correlated with children's cognitive scores have higher rates of cognitive inequality. The implication is that policies that would mitigate the effects of parents' attainment on children's outcomes would lead to a more equal society. But this does not tell us how important parents' attainment is (relative to other factors) or which policies might be most effective in breaking this link.

Recent research by Esping-Andersen (2004) suggests that preschool programs may be particularly consequential. Esping-Andersen (2004) shows that the Nordic countries have been the most successful in breaking the link between parental attainment and children's outcomes and makes the case that the provision of universal and high-quality child care has made the difference. As Esping-Andersen (2004) notes, the period when inequality in children's cognitive attainment decreased roughly corresponds to the period when universal child care came into place. And certainly the hypothesis that universal enrollment into high-quality child care leads to more equal outcomes than enrollment into care where the quality is correlated with parents' ability to pay makes good sense. However, it is possible that other things changed at the same time – other aspects of pre-school or school-age experience having to do with poverty, corporal punishment, teaching practices within schools – and that these other changes played at least some role. Without test scores on children at various ages, and samples of children who experienced different policy regimes, we can not know for certain what role preschool played and what role was played by other factors.

In a similar vein, in a recent review on 'Inequality in early childhood care and education' in the US, Marcia Meyers, Dan Rosenbaum, Chris Ruhm and I documented large disparities in preschool enrolment between children of less and more educated parents (as well as between children from low and higher income families) and argued that children from the most disadvantaged families are 'doubly disadvantaged' – less likely to receive stimulation and needed resources at home, and less likely to attend the type of care that we know promotes school readiness (Meyers *et al.*, 2004). If these children also attend lower-quality programs, even when they do attend preschools, then they could in fact be 'triply disadvantaged'. The logic of this argument is compelling, but does not tell us how large a role preschool care and education could play, how large a role could be played by other policies, and how much variation might remain even after our best policy efforts. Quantifying the impacts of policies and unpicking their influence on differences in child attainment at school entry is challenging

Recently, Katherine Magnuson and I conducted some rough estimates of how much early childhood education policy reforms could narrow the gaps in school readiness between minority and white children in the US (Magnuson and Waldfogel, forthcoming a). We concluded that early childhood education programs such as Head Start and universal prekindergarten are probably already playing an important role in narrowing gaps between Hispanic and white children, and between African-American and white children. We also concluded that the effect of program expansions will depend on the quality of the programs implemented as well as the children they reach. Our estimates indicate that reforms to current early education policies could reduce gaps in reading readiness at school entry by between zero and fifty-two per cent, depending on the policy scenario and the particular group involved. These analyses confirm that there is an important role for early childhood education policy to play, but that there is a role for other policies as well. There is no one magic bullet.

With these considerations in mind, this chapter reviews what we know from research about the early years and then critically assesses the policy framework in the UK and makes recommendations for next steps to improve social mobility and other outcomes in the early years.

What we know from research

Pregnancy and the first year of life

A host of studies have found that parental leave is associated with better maternal and child health, with specific findings for: lower maternal depression (Chatterji & Markowitz, 2004); lower infant mortality (Ruhm, 2000; Tanaka, forthcoming); fewer low birth-weight babies (Tanaka, forthcoming); more breast-feeding (Berger, Hill, and Waldfogel, forthcoming); and more use of preventive health care (Berger et al., forthcoming). The research is also clear that unpaid leave does not have the same protective effects (Ruhm, 2000; Tanaka, forthcoming), which makes sense, given that parents are less likely to use leave if it is not paid.

Research has also provided a clear set of findings with regard to parental employment and child care in the first year of life. The single most important finding, which cuts across virtually all studies that have been able to assess it, is the importance of quality of care – in particular, sensitivity and responsiveness to the child (see reviews in Shonkoff and Phillips, 2000; Smolensky and Gootman, 2003). The other clear finding is that maternal employment in the first year, particularly if begun early and full-time, is associated with poorer cognitive development and more behaviour problems, for at least some children (see Brooks-Gunn, Han, and Waldfogel, 2002 for the US; and Gregg, Washbrook, Propper, and Burgess, forthcoming for the UK; see also reviews in Shonkoff and Phillips, 2000; Smolensky and Gootman, 2003). These effects vary by the type and quality of child care, the quality of parental care, and family income. For example, in analyses of the ALSPAC cohort of children from the Bristol area, among families where mothers worked full-time in the first eighteen months, children had better outcomes if they were in formal (paid) care (Gregg et al., forthcoming).

Children aged one and two

Looking first at cognitive and behavioural outcomes, the over-riding message of the research is that quality of care matters (Blau, 2001; Shonkoff and Phillips, 2000; Smolensky and Gootman, 2003; Vandell and Wolfe, 2000). For young children, what defines quality is that the care they receive – whether from a parent or a non-parental caregiver – is sensitive and responsive to their individual needs. This type of process quality is hard (and expensive) to measure, as it requires in-person observation of the child and caregiver, so often researchers rely on more easily measured structural characteristics, such as caregiver education or caregiver-to-child ratio, which have been found to be associated with process quality and child outcomes.

The role of quality can be seen in the research on maternal employment and child care. The weight of the evidence suggests that there are no adverse effects of maternal employment on cognitive development when children are age one and two, but that there may be adverse effects on behaviour problems if children are in poor quality child care for long hours (Brooks-Gunn, Han, and Waldfogel, 2002; NICHD Early Child Care Research Network (ECCRN), 2003; Ruhm, 2004).

Does this mean that if the quality of care is good enough, there are no adverse effects on social and emotional development if children start care at the age of one or two? The evidence from high-quality interventions, which have been experimentally evaluated, suggests that the answer is yes. A large body of research from such experimental studies shows that high-quality child care for children in this age range produces cognitive gains, with no adverse effects on behaviours (Currie, 2001; Karoly et al., 1998; Waldfogel, 2002). Indeed, many of the programs' most lasting gains – reductions in delinquency and crime, reductions in teen births – were in the area of social and emotional development (Carneiro and Heckman, 2003). These experimental programs were mainly targeted to disadvantaged children, and produced the largest effects for the most disadvantaged. For example, the Infant Health and Development Program (IHDP), an early intervention program for low-birthweight children which provided centre-based care starting at the age of one, boosted IQ at age three by twenty points for children whose mothers had less than a high school education, ten points for children whose mothers had graduated high school only, and zero points for children whose mothers had graduated college (Brooks-Gunn et al., 1992; Ramey and Ramey, 2000). Centre-based programs for children in this age range also boost maternal education, employment, and earnings. For example, the Abecedarian program, an early intervention program that provided centre-based care to disadvantaged children starting in the first year of life, raised mothers' earnings by an average of $3,750 per year (Masse and Barnett, 2004).

Because the experimental programs were targeted to disadvantaged children, we lack experimental evidence as to whether child care for one or two year olds has adverse effects on behavioural outcomes for more advantaged children. As noted above, observational studies (such as NICHD ECCRN,

2003 and Sammons *et al.*, 2003) did find that children who entered care earlier had more behaviour problems. The NICHD ECCRN (2003) study was not able to pin down an age at which entry into child care would not pose this risk (most of their sample had entered non-parental child care in the first year of life, making it difficult to isolate large groups who did not begin child care until age two or three). The EPPE study (which I discuss further below) did address this question and found that the effects on behaviour problems were largest for children who began care before the age of two (Sammons *et al.*, 2003). But, there is a good deal of disagreement as to how consequential such behaviour problems are for children's school readiness or later success in life. While some argue that even a small elevation in behaviour problems should be of concern, others note that children who attended a lot of care from an early date do not typically have clinically meaningful levels of behaviour problems and that the behaviours they do show do not inhibit their school readiness or progress through school.

With regard to health outcomes, young children attending group child care do have more illnesses (Gordon, Kaestner, and Korenman, 2004; Meyers *et al.*, 2004). Safety is also a potential concern, particularly in low-quality care, although rates of injury and abuse are actually lower in child care than in children's own homes (Currie and Hotz, forthcoming; Waldfogel, in progress). Evidence from the US Early Head Start program suggests that involvement in child care may be protective in terms of reducing the use of physical punishment (spanking) by children's parents (Love *et al.*, 2002).

Children aged three to five

Again, to begin with effects on cognitive and behavioural outcomes, the research finds no adverse effects of maternal employment in these years on cognitive development, but some effects on child behaviours if children are in poor quality care for long hours (Brooks-Gunn *et al.*, 2002; NICHD ECCRN, 2003). Turning to child care, high-quality preschool programs for disadvantaged children produce substantial cognitive gains (Currie, 2001; Karoly *et al.*, 1998; Waldfogel, 2002). Such programs have no adverse effects on child behaviour outcomes and indeed have been found to reduce later problems such as crime (Carneiro and Heckman, 2003; Donohoe and Siegelman, 1998). Such programs may also boost mothers' education, employment, and earnings. Even run-of-the-mill preschool programs have been found to boost children's school readiness, although of course not as much as the high-quality model programs (NICHD ECCRN and Duncan, 2003; see also reviews in Magnuson and Waldfogel, forthcoming a; Meyers *et al.*, 2004). I discuss the most recent evidence on such programs below.

With regard to health outcomes, there is some evidence that maternal employment may have adverse effects on child health if it is not associated with income gains (Morris *et al.*, 2001). There is also evidence that maternal employment when children are aged three to five may lead to an increased risk of child obesity (Anderson *et al.*, 2003; Ruhm, 2003). There are some adverse effects of group child care on child health, and some concerns about safety, particularly in low-quality care (Meyers *et al.*, 2004). But child care may also be protective, reducing physical discipline (spanking) and domestic violence (Magnuson and Waldfogel, forthcoming b).

It is worth highlighting results from two recent large-scale studies that provide new evidence on the effects of preschool for three to five year old children. These studies are important because they examined programs that are widely available to children, and not just model or demonstration programs. In the US, the Early Childhood Longitudinal Study- Kindergarten Cohort (ECLS-K) is following a large cohort of children who were in kindergarten in the fall of 1998. Analyses of these children (Magnuson, Meyers, Ruhm, and Waldfogel, 2004; Magnuson, Ruhm, and Waldfogel, 2004) have found that preschool raises school readiness and also lowers retention (i.e., children being 'held back' and required to repeat kindergarten). In these analyses, preschool includes what parents call nursery school, preschool, day care, or prekindergarten (Head Start programs are categorised separately). Analyses that look at different types of preschool find that effects are particularly large for children who attended a pre-kindergarten program; these children score better in reading and math (effect size about 0.16 at school entry) and are about twenty-five per cent less likely to be retained (Magnuson, Meyers, Ruhm, and Waldfogel, 2004). Effects are larger and longer-lasting for disadvantaged children (children with less-educated parents, with families speaking a language other than English at home, or with low-income families or families on welfare). Effects are also larger for children who attended more hours of prekindergarten (full-day rather than half-day), although this finding was specific to prekindergarten (that is, more hours of other types of preschool programs were not found to confer added benefits). But longer hours in preschool (including prekindergarten) are also associated with more behaviour problems, although this is not the case for children who attended prekindergarten in the same school as their kindergarten (Magnuson, Ruhm, and Waldfogel, 2004).

Results from a large-scale study of children attending preschools in the UK are for the most part very similar. In the UK, the study of Effective Preschool Provision (EPPE) is following a large sample of children from preschool to school entry, and beyond. Analyses show that children who attend preschool enter school at a cognitive advantage (effect sizes 0.30 to 0.45; charts E3-E5 in Sammons *et al.*, 2002). The longer children had been in preschool, the greater the advantage (effect sizes for pre-reading, early number, and language range from 0.38 to 0.63 for those attending two to three years, or over three years; chart 4.1 in Sammons *et al.*, 2002). Children who began preschool at age two were ahead of children who began at age three, and maintained that gain at school entry. But this was not true for the small number of children who began before age two. The EPPE researchers have also found that children who attend preschool enter school with better social and behavioural development, except on the dimension of antisocial or worried behaviour where they score slightly worse (effect size 0.10; Sammons *et al.*, 2003). More detailed analyses indicate that both the type of care and time in care mattered: the only groups with significantly elevated levels of antisocial or worried behaviour consisted of children who attended local authority day care, or children who attended more than three years of preschool (this latter group tended to have been in group care prior to preschool and thus often had been in centre-based care starting before age two and sometimes as early as age one) (Sammons *et al.*, 2003, Table 5.4 and 5.5). For children who attended a type of care other than local authority day care, or who had attended three years or less, there were no significant effects on antisocial or worried behaviour. With regard to hours per day, in contrast to the findings for prekindergarten in the US but similar to the findings for other types of preschool programs, the EPPE study found no added cognitive benefits of attending full-day rather than half-day. Thus, the cognitive benefits of preschool were evident even if children only attended part-time.

Four additional findings from EPPE are worth highlighting because of their relevance to policy. First, as in the ECLS-K, the EPPE team found that disadvantaged children gained the most from attending preschool. In the case of EPPE, this applied to children at risk of being identified for special educational needs, children for whom English was an additional language, and children from some ethnic minority groups. Second, again similar to what was found in ECLS-K, the quality and effectiveness of care on offer currently in the UK is uneven. The EPPE study has produced very clear findings as to what types of care are most effective in boosting children's school readiness. For instance, centres that integrated care and education provision and nursery schools were found to be particularly effective, with especially beneficial effects for children from low-socioeconomic status families. So too were programs that had more highly qualified staff and managers (i.e, with level 5 qualifications). Third, EPPE found some indications that there may be composition effects. For instance, children were found to make more progress in pre-reading if they attended centres with more children from highly educated families. Fourth, EPPE provides some evidence that preschool experience can reduce differentials between children with different backgrounds. Thus, the EPPE group found that the impact of child, family, and home environment factors was weaker at school entry than it had been at age three for some of the cognitive outcomes (pre-reading and early numbers; Table 2.2. in Sammons *et al.*, 2002), although not for social and behavioural outcomes.

Parenting support

Parenting support programs are very diverse and the evidence on their effectiveness in changing parental behaviours and improving child outcomes is
very varied as well (see reviews in Brooks-Gunn and Markman, forthcoming; Desfarges, 2004; Gomby *et al.*, 1999; Harker and Kendall, 2003; Karoly
et al., 1998; Magnuson, 2004; Neuman and Dickinson, 2003; Sweet and
Appelbaum, 2004). With regard to cognitive outcomes, there is little evidence that parenting support programs in and of themselves improve children's school readiness, although there are exceptions in the area of early
literacy (for example, in the US, a program developed by Whitehurst that
emphasises dialogic reading has been found to raise children's language
scores (see Whitehurst *et al.*, 1994, 1999; Whitehurst and Lonigan, 1998),
while in the UK, the Peers Early Education Partnership (PEEP) program, a
home-based literacy program for families with three to five year olds was
found to improve school readiness (see Evangelou and Sylva, 2003). There
is also little evidence that parenting support programs improve social or
emotional outcomes for children (the exception here is programs specifically targeted to families with children with severe behaviour problems,
which have been found to lead to improvements; see Webster-Stratton,
1998; Webster-Stratton, Reid, and Hammond, 2001; Webster-Stratton and
Taylor, 2001). The area where parenting support programs for families
with young children have been found to be most effective is with regard to
health-related outcomes. For instance, high-quality home visiting programs
beginning in pregnancy and continuing post-birth have been found to
reduce the risk of child maltreatment (Karoly *et al.*, 1998).

One challenge in evaluating the effectiveness of parenting support programs is that often parenting support is offered in conjunction with other
types of support. In the early years, parenting support is often offered in
conjunction with centre-based care. Program designers believe that getting parents involved and supporting parents increases the effectiveness of
centre-based programs. But the fact that programs are combined makes it
difficult to identify the unique effects of parenting support as distinct from
the centre-based care. The few studies that have specifically tackled this
question have produced mixed results (see reviews in Brooks-Gunn and
Markman, forthcoming; Ramey and Ramey, 2000; Sweet and Appelbaum,
2004). In sum, then, the evidence in this area is weak, but the jury is still
out as to the role that parenting support programs might play in the UK
context.

Current policy framework

Early years policy is changing rapidly, as policy makers have recognised its
potential to advance social mobility and other desired outcomes. Policy
makers have been quick to respond to the research in this area and have

drawn on it in designing new policy initiatives (see, for example, the Five-Year Strategy for Children and Learners, Department for Education and Skills, 2004). (A comprehensive package of further reforms – a ten-year strategy for childcare – was published in December 2004, shortly after this paper was written; see HM Treasury, 2004).

Here, I briefly review the policy framework in the UK as of November 2004. Understanding this context and how well it conforms to what we know from research is necessary before moving on to discussing next steps for policy.

Parental leave

Maternity leave provisions have been expanded in recent years and now offer twelve months of job-protected leave to new mothers who were in work prior to the birth and meet qualifying conditions, but only six months of these are paid (six weeks at ninety per cent of prior earnings and the other twenty weeks at a flat rate, currently a hundred pounds a week). In addition, the qualifying service period has been reduced so that more mothers who were in work qualify. Mothers who were not in work pre-birth may receive other forms of support if they are low-income, like other low-income families with children. In addition, the Sure Start Maternity Grant, introduced in 2000, offers a one-time payment (currently, £500) to low-income new mothers to help with the purchase of essential items for the baby. All families with a newborn benefit from a 'baby tax credit' introduced in April 2002, and all babies born since September 2002 receive a £250 endowment in the Child Trust Fund, with a higher endowment (totalling £500) for low-income families.

Surveys of new parents consistently find that mothers tend to take as much leave as they can, but that income matters: lower-income mothers tend to return when paid leave ends, while higher-income mothers tend to return later, when the period of job-protected leave ends (Burgess *et al.*, 2002; Hudson *et al.*, 2004; author's estimates from Millennium Cohort Survey).

Statutory paternity leave (two weeks, paid at the same flat rate as statutory maternity pay) was introduced in April 2003. Survey evidence indicates that prior to that, only about half of new fathers worked for firms that offered paternity or parental leave (author's estimates from Millennium Cohort Survey). A high share of these fathers – over eighty per cent – made use of this leave. Fathers also use other types of leave (sick leave, annual leave and so on) to take time off after the birth of a child. Overall, seventy-five per cent of new dads take some leave, with leave more likely if the child is a first-born. But again, income matters: fathers are more likely to take leave when they have higher incomes. The current situation is better, in that all fathers now have the right to two weeks of statutory paternity leave. However, it is likely that income differentials in the use of leave persist.

The UK also has a parental leave statute introduced in 1999 that allows parents to take up to thirteen weeks unpaid leave sometime between the birth of a child and the child's fifth birthday (this is extended to eighteen weeks which can be taken up to the child's eighteenth birthday in the case of children with disabilities). There is no statutory pay for this leave, but employees may use paid leave from other sources such as annual leave (if available). Awareness and use of parental leave is apparently fairly low (see, for instance, Hudson *et al.*, 2004, who found that only twenty-five per cent of new parents in their survey of families with a new birth in January 2001 were aware of the availability of parental leave).

A newer initiative (implemented in April 2003) is the right for parents of young children (or children with disabilities) to request to work part-time or flexible hours. According to evaluations one year after the policy was implemented (Camp, 2004; Maternity Alliance, 2004; Work Foundation, 2004), there is apparently high awareness of this policy and high take-up, particularly among mothers; however, not all requests are granted, and some employers argue that this benefit should not be limited to parents with young children, as this has the potential to create equity problems in the workplace.

Child care and education for the under threes

There have been many initiatives to improve access to care and quality of care both for the under threes and for older preschool age children, with particular attention to the disadvantaged. These include the National Child Care Strategy, Sure Start, Children's Centres, Early Excellence Centres, Neighbourhood Nurseries, and Children's Centres. However, places are not guaranteed for the under threes, as they are for children age three and four, although there is a pilot initiative to provide centre-based care for disadvantaged two year olds.

We know little about the quality of care for the under threes. Provision is very diverse, and often informal. Among children under the age of one, thirty-seven per cent are in child care or education and the vast majority of this is informal (thirty per cent of under ones are in informal care versus seven per cent in formal care (author's estimates from the Millennium Cohort Survey)). Among children under the age of two, seventy-eight per cent are in child care or education, but again much is informal (thirty-six per cent use informal only, twenty-nine per cent a mix of formal and informal, and thirteen per cent formal only) (Woodland *et al.*, 2002). Care for children in this age range is expensive: full-time care for a child under two averages £134 a week for nursery and £120 a week for childminder) and parents bear a large share of the costs (about seventy-five per cent) (Daycare Trust, 2004).

A publicly-funded part-time nursery place is now guaranteed for all three and four year olds. Participation rates are very high – with ninety-six per cent of three or four year olds attending during the prior week (Fitgerald *et al.*, 2002; Bell and Finch, 2004). Rates are lower for children of manual workers (ninety-three per cent), low-income families (ninety-three per cent), and ethnic minorities (ninety per cent), and these children attend different types of care (nursery classes, rather than playgroups or pre-schools) although less so than they did formerly (Fitzgerald *et al.*, 2002; Stewart, forthcoming).

We also know something about parents' views. According to the *6th Survey of Parents of Three & Four Year Olds*, conducted from the summer of 2001 to the spring of 2002 (Bell and Finch, 2004), just over half of parents feel there are not enough nursery education places in their local area, and about forty per cent feel there is not enough information provided to help parents choose a place (this latter problem is particularly likely to be reported by parents of younger children). However, only fifteen per cent of parents feel their child is getting too little education, a significant improvement over prior years (this share was twenty-three per cent in 1997 and nineteen per cent in 2001). With regard to multiple arrangements, a quarter of children attend more than one provider, although most parents say this is not a problem. Overall, a quarter of parents surveyed in 2000 and 2001 said cost restricted how much nursery education their child received (thirty per cent of those with incomes below £10,000 as opposed to twenty-three per cent of those with incomes of £30,000 or more) (Fitzgerald *et al.*, 2002). Among those not using care at all, about half would have liked to (eleven per cent said cost was a factor; forty-five per cent could not find a place or their child was too young). And, among those not using care five days a week, twenty-eight per cent said this was because they could not afford more care.

Parenting support

Parenting support is provided through several large-scale government programs, as well as through numerous smaller-scale or private projects. For instance, Sure Start, the government's program for young children living in the poorest communities, has a large parenting support component, which includes home-visiting, parent education, and parent support groups. An evaluation of Sure Start is underway (for preliminary findings, see National Evaluation of Sure Start, 2004; Stewart, forthcoming). In the voluntary sector, programs such as Home Start provide supportive services to parents of children under the age of five, delivered through networks of community-based volunteers; however, nearly half of parents say that they do not know where to go for support in their area (Harker and Kendall, 2003).

In the following sections, I draw on what we know from research to identify key next steps for policy in the early years, keeping in mind the several objectives of policy: to promote social mobility by improving child outcomes in the areas of cognitive development, social and emotional development, and health; while also promoting (or at least not adversely affecting) social inclusion, poverty reduction, parental employment, parental choice, and gender equity. In some instances, these objectives may be at odds, but it is important to keep them all in the frame so that where there are trade-offs, these can be explicitly considered.

It is easy to recommend a host of policies but of course, all policies have costs, and it is necessary to prioritise among them. For this reason, I list recommended next steps in order of priority, and also offer some descriptive information as to likely costs and benefits of the highest-priority items. However, a full cost-benefit analysis is beyond the scope of this paper. (For examples of recent cost-benefit analyses in this area, see Heckman and Masterov, 2004b; PricewaterhouseCoopers, 2004).

Extend parental leave

Given the evidence as to the health benefits of paid maternity leave and the evidence that low-income women tend to return to work when paid leave ends, the first priority in the parental leave area is to extend paid leave to the end of the first year of life, so that lower-income families can take advantage of it. Specifically, this would entail an additional twenty-six weeks of maternity leave, which could be paid at a flat rate (the current rate is a hundred pounds a week) and could be pro-rated if a mother returns to work part-time. Consideration should also be given to improving financial support for low-income mothers who were not in work pre-birth, as they currently receive little support above and beyond that provided to low-income families with older children.

However, the extended leave need not be limited to mothers (which is why I use the term parental leave; see also Moss and Deven, 1999). Particularly as leave extends from six to twelve months, there is no strong reason to favor maternal care over paternal care. And there are other reasons (such as gender equity) for making leave extensions gender neutral. Thus, paid leave of up to twelve months should be available to either the mother or father, with parents having the choice as to how to divide the leave between them. Extending paid parental leave to twelve months will be costly, as it would require an additional six months' pay to mothers on leave (or fathers, if they elect to use it in place of mothers). And, if mothers take the majority of leave, extending leave could have costs in terms of negative repercussions on the careers of the women taking the extra leave, hiring or pay for women overall, and gender equity in the home or labour market (although these risks would be lessened if men also had the option to take the leave). However, the benefits would be very substantial: reduced infant mortality (extending paid leave from six to twelve months is estimated to reduce overall infant mortality by 6.8 per cent and post-neonatal mortality by 10.5 per cent; Gregg and Waldfogel, forthcoming; Tanaka, forthcoming); improved child cognitive and social and emotional development; longer breast-feeding; and improved maternal and child health. In addition, extending parental leave would produce savings in child care costs, and would be responsive to what parents say they want.

The second priority, given the evidence as to benefits of leaves that extend beyond the first year of life as well as evidence as to possible adverse effects of long hours of non-maternal child care on behaviour problems, is to consider extending job-protected leave beyond the first year, with some financial support so that low-income families can take advantage of it. This might entail an additional twenty-six or fifty-two weeks of leave, which could be paid at a flat rate, again pro-rated if the mother returned part-time, or could be supported through other changes to the tax and benefit system, for example, through early childhood benefits or other benefits targeted to families with young children (discussed further below).

Third, it is important to monitor the April 2003 initiatives that gave parents of young children the right to request part-time and flexible hours and that gave fathers paternity leave rights, and to strengthen these if necessary. Research on these initiatives is still underway, but the research to date suggests that expansions are likely to be needed, to promote child well-being and also to respond to issues of parental choice and gender equity.

Improve the quality of care and education for the under threes

As we saw above, one of the clearest messages from research is the importance of the quality of care that children receive, particularly in the first few years of life. But the research is also clear that there is no one-size-fits-all type of care that is best for all children in this age range. Thus, there are two high priorities for next steps for this age group.

First, there is a need for a more flexible package of support for parents, to give them a better set of choices in the first two to three years. Not all families want to use centre-based care for children under the age of two or three, and for some children less intensive forms of provision might be more suitable, particularly during the period between their first and second birthday. One very attractive option is early childhood benefits – cash grants (these could be fifty to seventy pounds a week) that families can use for parental care or child care or a mixture of the two (Waldfogel, 2001). Such benefits would ideally be provided universally but could also be implemented on a targeted basis, for low-income families. Obviously, such a program would be costly and could induce more mothers to stay home, undermining efforts to promote parental employment and gender equity (although Duncan and Magnuson (2003) argue that the labour supply effects would likely be small). However, flexible supports allow parents to make a choice between parental care, non-parental care, or a mix of the two (i.e. working part-time and caring part-time, or splitting child care between parents). If parents elected to provide some care themselves at least part-time, this would yield savings in child care costs. And early childhood benefits, particularly if targeted to low-income families, could boost incomes and relieve financial hardship, leading to improved child outcomes (Duncan and Magnuson, 2003).

Second, there is a need for continued support for initiatives to improve access to care and quality of care, particularly centre-based care starting at age two for the most disadvantaged children, either through quality-linked subsidies or direct provision. The benefits of such a policy are clear, in terms of cognitive gains to children at greatest risk of school failure and also employment effects for their mothers. There may be other benefits to children and families as well (e.g. reductions in spanking and domestic violence).

However, there are also trade-offs and tough decisions to be made here. High-quality centre-based care is costly. Targetting such care to low-income children will save money and also reach the group likely to gain the largest benefits, but if other children do not use the care, it could become segregated or stigmatised and its quality could suffer. Thus, there is a need for creative policies that bring in a mix of children. For instance, spaces in new centres could be made available to higher-income children on a fee-paying basis.

There is also the challenge of how to raise quality and how to ensure that children are placed into good-quality care. As noted earlier, measuring process quality is difficult and expensive. But we know a lot from research about what structural features of care are linked with better process quality and better outcomes for children (see for instance NICHD ECCRN, 2002), and it is possible to design initiatives that boost those aspects of quality, by for example linking higher payments to providers with higher education levels and lower child-to-caregiver ratios, or only funding providers who meet specified education levels and child-to-caregiver ratios.

Finally, there is also the worry that starting children in care too early might lead to behaviour problems, at least for some. But here too quality is central as is the number of hours children are in care. My reading of the evidence is that most children can benefit from at least part-time care starting at the age of two, without adverse effects on social or emotional development. The case is most compelling for disadvantaged children, for whom the cognitive benefits are the largest. But a case can be made for offering at least a part-time place to all two-year olds whose parents want one. By this age, most parents want their child to have at least some exposure to other children and some experience in an early learning setting (and many parents as a practical matter need at least part-time child care while they are at work). Guaranteeing at least a part-time place to all two-year olds would support that choice and would also help equalise the quality of care that children from different backgrounds experience.

A third, less immediate priority but nevertheless important to pursue, is further research on the quality of care currently offered to children under age three. As discussed above, we know too little about this and this is a crucial gap, given what we know about how much quality matters.

Develop a more integrated system of high-quality care and education for three to fives

Government policy has already done much to improve care and education for three to five year olds, but there are three additional steps that policy-makers should take for this age group. The three steps are inter-related, and equally important.

- One is to raise preschool quality, whether through tighter standards or direct provision. The goal should be to provide a high-quality place for each child, on at least a half-time basis.

- A second is to build an easier and more generous system of subsidies for 'wrap-around' and out-of-school care for low-income families. Low-income families should be guaranteed that, if they are working, child care will be free or affordable. And the burden of paperwork should be shifted to providers, and away from parents.

- Third, there needs to be greater integration of nursery or school and wrap-around or out-of-school care. Too often, families bear the burden of having to piece together different provision, in different locations. The system of care and education needs to work to make that provision more seamless, and easier from the perspective of the family.

Building a better system of care and education will be costly – it will require more money for directors and teachers, subsidies for the lowest-income families, and new staff to coordinate provision. However, we know that better quality care pays dividends – gains in cognitive development, social and emotional development, and maternal employment. And efforts are already underway in each of these areas (see overviews in Cohen *et al.*, 2004; Stewart, forthcoming). Serious attention is being paid to the issue of quality in the child care workforce. Options to extend child care support for the lowest-income families are being studied. And Children's Centres are being rolled out nationwide, with part of their mission being to provide just this coordinating role. The issues here are complex but the key lesson from research is that quality needs to be central to any expanded child care initiative.

The provision of parenting support cuts across many of the areas discussed above. For instance, extensions in parental leave provide support for parental time with children and thus are a form of parenting support. So too are expansions in Children's Centres, which will help parents locate and access high-quality child care as well as other services for their family. What further steps should be taken to enhance parenting support, given what we know from the research? Answering this question is difficult, because although research has shown that parenting matters, and that programs can improve parenting, the links between programs and improved outcomes for children have not often been established. Further research should be the top priority in the form of a set of studies that evaluate the impact of carefully designed interventions on desired child outcomes. The evidence from an early literacy program such as PEEP is encouraging and should be used to inform further experimentation. Children's Centres can and should be actively involved in these efforts so that model interventions can be rolled out quickly if they prove to be effective.

Conclusions

As we have seen, early years policies must address multiple outcomes, promoting social mobility and improved child well-being, while also promoting other social goals – social inclusion, poverty reduction, parental employment, parental choice, and gender equity.

The bottom line message from research on the early years is that quality matters. This leads to a clear policy conclusion: policies should aim to support parents both in providing good-quality care themselves, and in arranging good-quality child care.

We also know a good deal from research about what quality means, and about what types of experiences are best for children. The research points to some clear next steps in early years policy. These include:

- extending paid parental leave to twelve months;

- offering a more flexible package of supports to families with children under the age of two or three;

- providing high-quality centre-based care to two year olds, starting with the most disadvantaged; and

- providing a more integrated system of high-quality care and education for three to five year olds.

In focusing on the early years, I do not mean to suggest that only early years policies are important. As I said at the outset, the evidence suggests that about half the gap in school achievement is already present at school entry. While providing a powerful reason for intervening in the preschool years, this statement implies that the gap widens further after school entry. An early years intervention cannot inoculate children against future disadvantage. Proven early years policies can go a long way toward closing achievement gaps and promoting social mobility, and they deserve all the support we can muster for them. But so too do some policies for school-age children and youth and we should not pit one against the other. It is clear from the research that combating disadvantage and promoting social mobility requires sustained efforts that begin before birth, and continue throughout childhood and adolescence.

Afterword

Shortly after this paper was written, the government announced an ambitious and far-reaching ten year childcare strategy 'Choice for parents, the best start for children: a ten year strategy for childcare' (HM Treasury, 2004). The ten year strategy is based on the research evidence and includes a comprehensive set of investments in the early years, along the lines of those recommended here, as well as a set of enhanced supports for families with school-age children. The strategy also includes a detailed timeline and set of interim objectives for making progress toward the ten-year goals.

As an American academic, I applaud the commitment the British government and the British policy community have made to meeting the challenge to combat disadvantage and promote social mobility. The ten year strategy for childcare represents a major investment in improving the quality of care for children. I can only hope that one day soon we will see such a commitment in my own country.

References

Alakeson, V. (2004) *A 2020 Vision for Early Years: Extending choice; improving life chances* London: Social Market Foundation

Anderson, P., Butcher, K. and Levine, P. (2003) 'Maternal Employment and Overweight Children' *Journal of Health Economics* 22(3):477-504

Bell, A. and Finch, S. (2004) *6th Survey of Parents of Three & Four Year Old Children and Their Use of Early Years Services* Report by National Centre for Social Research for the Department for Education and Skills. Available at www.dfes. gov.uk/research/

Berger, L., Hill, J. and Waldfogel, J. (forthcoming) 'Maternity Leave, Early Maternal Employment, and Child Health and Development in the US' Forthcoming in *Economic Journal*

Blanden, J., Gregg, P. and Machin, S. (2003) 'Changes in Educational Inequality' London: Centre for Economic Performance

Blau, D. (2001) *The Child Care Problem* New York: Russell Sage Foundation Press

Brooks-Gunn, J., Gross, R.T., Kraemer, H.C., Spiker, D. and Shapiro, S. (1992) 'Enhancing the Cognitive Outcomes of Low Birth Weight Premature Infants: For Whom Is Intervention Most Effective?' *Pediatrics* 89(8):1209-1215

Brooks-Gunn, J., Han, W. and Waldfogel, J. (2002) 'Maternal Employment and Child Cognitive Outcomes in the First Three Years of Life: The NICHD Study of Early Child Care' *Child Development* 73(4):1052-1072

Brooks-Gunn, J. and Markman, L.B. (forthcoming) 'The Contribution of Parenting to Ethnic and Racial Gaps in School Readiness' Forthcoming in *The Future of Children* 15(1), Special Issue on 'School Readiness: Closing Racial and Ethnic Gaps'

Burgess, S., Gregg, P., Propper, C., Washbrook, E. and the ALSPAC Study Team (2002) 'Maternity Rights and Mothers' Return to Work' *CMPO Working Paper* 02/055, University of Bristol

Camp, C. (2004) *Right to Request Flexible Working: Review of impact in first year of legislation* Report for the Department of Trade and Industry

Carneiro, P. and Heckman, J.J. (2003) 'Human Capital Policy' in Friedman, B.W. (ed.) *Inequality in America: What role for human capital policies?* Cambridge, MA: MIT Press

Chatterji, P. and Markowitz, S. (2004). 'Does the Length of Maternity Leave Affect Maternal Health?' *NBER Working Paper* 10206. Cambridge, MA: National Bureau for Economic Research

Cohen, B., Moss, P., Petrie, P. and Wallace, J. (2004) *A New Deal for Children? Re-Forming education and care in England, Scotland, and Sweden* Bristol: The Policy Press

Currie, J. (2001) 'Early Childhood Intervention Programs: What Do We Know?' *Journal of Economic Perspectives* 15:213-238

Currie, J. and Hotz, V.J. (forthcoming) 'Accidents Will Happen? Unintentional childhood injuries and the effects of child care regulations' Forthcoming in *Journal of Health Economics*

Daycare Trust (2004) 'Childcare Costs Rise to Record Levels' Available from www.daycaretrust.org.uk

Department for Education and Skills (2004) *Five Year Strategy for Children and Learners* London: HMSO

Desfarges, C. with Abouchaar, A. (2003) 'The Impact of Parental Involvement, Parental Support, and Family Education on Pupil Achievements and Adjustment: A Literature Review' *Research Report* 433. London: Department for Education and Skills

Donohoe, J. and Siegelman, P. (1998) 'Allocating Resources among Prisons and Social Programs in the Battle against Crime' *Journal of Legal Studies* 27(1):1-43

Duncan, G. and Magnuson, K. (2003) 'Promoting the Healthy Development of Young Children' pp. 16-39 in Sawhill I (ed.) *One Percent for the Kids: New policies, brighter futures for America's children* Washington, DC: Brookings Institution Press

Esping-Anderson, G.(2004) 'Untying the Gordian Knot of Social Inheritance' *Research in Social Stratification and Mobility* 21:115-139

Evangelou, M. and Sylva, K. (2003) 'The Effects of the Peers Early Education Partnership (PEEP) on Children's Developmental Progress' Brief RB489. London: Department for Education and Skills

Feinstein, L. (2003) 'Inequality in the Early Cognitive Development of British Children in the 1970 Cohort' *Economica* 70(227):73-98

Fitzgerald, R., Finch, S. Blake, M. Perry, J. and Bell, A. (2002) *5th Survey of Parents of Three and Four Year Old Children and Their Use of Early Years Services (Summer 2000 to Spring 2001)* Research Brief 351, prepared by the National Centre for Social Research for the Department for Education and Skills. Available at www.dfes.gov.uk/research/

Gomby, D., Culross, P.L. and Behrman, R. (1999) 'Home Visiting: Recent Program Evaluations – Analysis and Recommendations' *The Future of Children* 9:4-26

Gordon, R., Kaestner, R. and Korenman, S. (2004) 'Effects of Maternal Employment on Child Injuries and Infectious Diseases' Chicago, IL: University of Illinois at Chicago, Department of Economics

Gregg, P. and Waldfogel, J. (forthcoming) 'Introduction to Symposium on Parental Leave, Early Maternal Employment, and Child Outcomes' *The Economic Journal*

Gregg, P., Propper, C. and Burgess, S. (forthcoming)

Gregg, P., Washbrook, E., Propper, C. and Burgess, S. (forthcoming) 'The Effects of a Mother's Return to Work Decision on Child Development in the UK' The *Economic Journal*

Harker, L. and Kendall, L. (2003) *An Equal Start: Improving support during pregnancy and the first 12 months* London: ippr

Heckman, J.J. and Lochner, L. (2000) 'Rethinking Education and Training Policy: Understanding the sources of skill formation in a modern economy' pp. 47-86 in Danziger, S. and Waldfogel, J. (eds.) *Securing the Future: Investing in children from birth to college* New York: Russell Sage Foundation Press

Heckman, J. and Masterov, D. (2004a) 'Skill Policies for Scotland' Available at http://lily.src.uchicago.edu/~dvmaster/Scotland.html

Heckman, J. and Masterov, D. (2004b) 'The Productivity Argument for Investing in Young Children' Working Paper 5, Invest in Kids Working Group, Committee for Economic Development. Available at http//jenni.uchicago.edu/Invest/

Heckman, J, and Wax, A. (2004) 'Home Alone' *Wall Street Journal* 23.1.04, p. A14

HM Treasury (2004) *Choice for Parents, the Best Start for Children: A ten year strategy for childcare* London: HMSO

Hudson, M., Lissenburgh, S. and Sahin-Dikmen, M. (2004) *Maternity and Paternity Rights in Britain 2002: Survey of parents* A Report by the Policy Studies Institute for the Department for Work and Pensions and the Department of Trade and Industry. London: HMSO

Karoly, L., Greenwood, P., Everingham, S., Hoube, J., Kilburn, R., Rydell, P., Sanders, M. and Chiesa, J. (1998) *Investing in Our Children: What we know and don't know about the costs and benefits of early childhood interventions* Santa Monica: RAND

Love, J.M., Eliason-Kisker, E., Ross, C.M., Schochet, P.Z., Brooks-Gunn, J. and Paulsell, D. (2002) *Making a Difference in the Lives of Infants and Toddlers and Their Families: The impacts of early head start* Washington, DC: US Department of Health and Human Services, Administration for Children and Families

Magnuson, K. (2004) 'Parenting Interventions: How to spend the marginal dollar?' Presentation to ippr/HM Treasury Conference on Life Chances and Social Mobility: 'Where Do We Spend the Marginal Pound?' 30.3.04

Magnuson, K., Meyers, M., Ruhm, C. and Waldfogel, J. (2004) 'Inequality in Preschool Education and School Readiness' *American Educational Research Journal* 41(1):115-157

Magnuson, K., Ruhm, C. and Waldfogel, J. (2004) 'Does Prekindergarten Improve School Preparation and Performance?' Revised version of NBER Working Paper 10452, Cambridge, MA

Magnuson, K. and Waldfogel, J. (forthcoming a) 'Early Childhood Care and Education, and Ethnic and Racial Gaps in Readiness at School Entry' *The Future of Children* 15(1) Special Issue on 'School Readiness: Closing racial and ethnic gaps'

Magnuson, K. and Waldfogel, J. (forthcoming b) 'Pre-School Enrollment and Parents' Use of Physical Discipline' *Infant and Child Development*

Masse, L.N. and Barnett, W.S. (2004) *A Benefit Cost Analysis of the Abecedarian Early Childhood Intervention* New Brunswick, NJ: National Institute for Early Education Research

Maternity Alliance (2004) *Happy Anniversary? The right to request flexible work one year on* London: Maternity Alliance

Meyers, M., Rosenbaum, D. Ruhm, C. and Waldfogel, J. (2004) 'Inequality in Early Childhood Care and Education: What do we know?' in Neckerman, K. (ed.) *Social Inequality* New York: Russell Sage Foundation Press

Morris, P.A., Huston, A.C., Duncan, G.J., Crosby, D.A. and Bos, J.M. (2001) *How Welfare and Work Policies Affect Children: A synthesis of research* New York: Manpower Demonstration Research Corporation

Moss, P. and Deven, F. (eds) *Parental Leave: Progress or pitfall?* Brussels: CBGS

National Evaluation of Sure Start (2004) 'The Impact of Sure Start Local Programmes on Child Development and Family Functioning: A report on preliminary findings' available from the Institute for the Study of Children, Families and Social Issues, Birkbeck College, University of London

Neuman, S. and Dickinson, D. (eds.) (2003) *Handbook of Early Literacy Research* New York: Guilford

NICHD Early Child Care Research Network (2002) 'Child Care Structure > Process > Outcome: Direct and Indirect Effects of Child-Care Quality on Young Children's Development' *Psychological Science* 13:199-206

NICHD Early Child Care Research Network (2003) 'Does Amount of Time Spent in Child Care Predict Socioemotional Adjustment during the Transition to Kindergarten?' *Child Development* 74(4):976-1005

NICHD Early Child Care Research Network and Greg Duncan (2003) 'Modeling the Impacts of Child Care Quality on Children's Preschool Cognitive Development' *Child Development* 74:1454-1475

Phillips, M., Crouse, J. and Ralph, J. (1998) 'Does the Black-White Test Score Gap Widen after Children Enter School?' pp. 229-272 in Jencks, C. and Phillips, M. (eds.) *The Black-White Test Score Gap* Washington, DC: Brookings Institution Press

PricewaterhouseCoopers (2004) *Universal Early Education and Care in 2020: Costs, Benefits, and Funding Options* A Report for Daycare Trust and the Social Market Foundation. Available from Daycare Trust, PricewaterhouseCoopers, and Social Market Foundation

Ramey, C.T. and Ramey, S.L. (2000) 'Early Childhood Experiences and Developmental Competence' pp. 122-152 in Danziger, S. and Waldfogel, J. (eds.) *Securing the Future: Investing in children from birth to college* New York: Russell Sage Foundation Press

Rothstein, R. (2003) *Class and Schools: Using social, economic, and educational reform to close the black-white achievement gap* Washington, DC: Economic Policy Institute

Rouse, C., Brooks-Gunn, J. and McLanahan, S. (forthcoming) 'Ethnic and Racial Gaps in School Readiness' *The Future of Children* 15(1), Special Issue on 'School Readiness: Closing racial and ethnic gaps'

Ruhm, C. (2000) 'Parental Leave and Child Health' *Journal of Health Economics* 19(6):931-960

Ruhm, C. (2003) 'Maternal Employment and Adolescent Development' Mimeo, University of North Carolina at Greensboro

Ruhm, C. (2004) 'Parental Employment and Child Cognitive Development' *Journal of Human Resources* 39(1):155-192

Sammons, P., Sylva, K., Melhuish, E., Siraj-Blatchford, I., Taggart, B. and Elliot, K. (2002) 'Measuring the Impact of Pre-School on Children's Cognitive Progress over the Pre-School Period' Technical Paper 8a, The Effective Provision of Pre-School Provision (EPPE) Project. London: Institute of Education, University of London

Sammons, P., Sylva, K., Melhuish, E., Siraj-Blatchford, I., Taggart, B. and Elliot, K. (2003) 'Measuring the Impact of Pre-School on Children's Social/Behavioural Development over the Pre-School Period' Technical Paper 8b, The Effective Provision of Pre-School Provision (EPPE) Project. London: Institute of Education, University of London

Shonkoff, J.P. and Phillips, D.A. (eds.) (2000) *From Neurons to Neighbourhoods: The science of early childhood developmen* Washington, DC: National Academy Press

Smolensky, E. and Gootman, J. (eds.) (2003) *Working Families and Growing Kids: Caring for children and adolescents* Washington, DC: National Academy Press

Stewart, K. (forthcoming) 'Towards an Equal Start? Addressing childhood poverty and deprivation' in Hills, J. and Stewart, K. (eds.) *A More Equal Society? New Labour, poverty, inequality, and exclusion* Bristol: Policy Press

Sweet, M.A. and Appelbaum, M.I. (2004) 'Is Home Visiting an Effective Strategy? A meta-analytic review of home visiting programs for families with young children' *Child Development* 75(5):1435-1456

Tanaka, S. (forthcoming) 'Parental Leave and Child Health Across OECD Countries' *The Economic Journal*

Vandell, D.L. and Wolfe, B. (2002) *Child Care Quality: Does it matter and does it need to be improved?* Washington, DC: Office of the Assistant Secretary for Planning and Evaluation, U.S. Department of Health and Human Services

Waldfogel, J. (2001) 'What Other Nations Do: International policies toward parental leave and child care' *The Future of Children* 11(4):99-111

Waldfogel, J. (2002) 'Child Care, Women's Employment, and Child Outcomes' *Journal of Population Economics* 15:527-548

Waldfogel, J. (in progress) *Getting it Right: Meeting the needs of children when parents work* Manuscript in progress

Webster-Stratton, C. (1998) 'Preventing Conduct Problems in Head Start Children: Strengthening Parenting Competences' *Journal of Consulting and Clinical Psychology* 66:715-730

Webster-Stratton, C., Reid, J. and Hammond, M. (2001) 'Preventing Conduct Problems, Promoting Social Competence: A parent and child training partnership in head start' *Journal of Child Clinical Psychology* 30:283

Webster-Stratton, C. and Taylor, T. (2001) 'Nipping Early Risk Factors in the Bud: Preventing Substance Abuse, Delinquency, and Violence in Adolescence through Interventions Targeted at Young Children (0-8 Years)' *Prevention Science* 2:165-192

Whitehurst, G. and Lonigan, C.J. (1998) 'Child Development and Emergent Literacy' *Child Development* 69:848-872

Whitehurst, G., Zevenbergen, A.A., Crone, D.A., Schultz, M.D., Velting, O.N. and Fischel,J.E. (1994) 'Outcomes of an Emergent Literacy Intervention in Head Start' *Journal of Educational Psychology* 86:542

Whitehurst, G., Zevenbergen, A.A., Crone, D.A., Schultz, M.D., Velting, O.N. and Fischel, J.E. (1999) 'Outcomes of an Emergent Literacy Intervention from Head Start through Second Grade' *Journal of Educational Psychology* 91:261-272

Woodland, S., Miller, M. and Tipping, S. (2002) *Repeat Study of Parents' Demand for Childcare* Research Brief 348, prepared by the National Centre for Social Research for the Department for Education and Skills. Available at www.dfes.gov.uk/research/

Work Foundation (2004) 'Lowest Paid Losing Out in Right to Request Flexible Working' 5.4.04 Press Release, available at www.theworkfoundation.com

4 Social inequalities and education policy in England
Alice Sullivan and Geoff Whitty

Education is a key determinant of life chances in industrialised societies (Shavit and Blossfeld, 1993), and educational credentials are an important intervening link between social origins and occupational destinations (Halsey *et al.*, 1980). But the importance of education is not limited to its impact on labour market outcomes. Education has been linked to a broad range of indicators of quality of life, from health to civic participation (Schuller *et al.*, 2004).

This chapter deals with educational differences in terms of social class, gender and ethnicity. These are key socially-structured ascribed identities affecting children's educational experiences and outcomes. It examines the impact of these categories together and explores significant interactions between them. It then discusses the economic, social and cultural factors underlying these inequalities, and the impact of current government policies.

The roles of the home, the school and the wider society in determining socially-structured differences in educational outcomes are examined. The chapter considers what impact government policy can realistically be expected to have on educational inequalities, and what types of policies may be most productive. A key point to emerge from this overview is that the continuing impact of social class on educational outcomes should not be ignored either by policymakers or by researchers. There is a need for greater honesty in the presentation of policy-relevant research findings, in particular to acknowledge the limits of what one can infer from data which does not contain adequate measures of children's socio-economic backgrounds.

Sociological perspectives on educational differences between groups

Social class

The existence of large social class differentials in educational attainment is well established for all industrialised societies. Although there is evidence that educational reforms have reduced differences in rates of educational participation between the social classes (Hellevik, 1997; Jonsson and Mills, 1993b; Jonsson and Mills, 1993a), the association between social class and educational outcomes remains in tact. In addition, the labour market is not 'class blind', as occupational attainment can be shown to be associated with social class of origin, independently of educational attainment and test scores (Marshall and Swift 1996; Breen and Goldthorpe 1999).

Social class inequalities in tested ability emerge at a young age and increase steadily over time (Fogelman, 1983; Fogelman and Goldstein, 1976; Feinstein, 2003; Douglas, 1964). Furthermore, later educational transitions (such as the transition to higher education) in Britain appear to be largely determined by prior academic attainment (Galindo-Rueda et al., 2004), which suggests that social class inequalities do need to be tackled early on.

Social class is defined in terms of occupational categories, but high social class status is associated with social and cultural privilege, as well as economic privilege. Sociologists often explain social class differences in educational attainment in terms of three forms of capital: economic capital, cultural capital and social capital.

Despite the introduction of universal free and compulsory schooling, financial resources still give an advantage in pursuing educational attainment. Well-off parents can afford better schools for their children, by buying either private schooling or housing in a good catchment area. In addition, many pupils receive private tuition (Ireson and Rushforth, 2004). Educational resources such as a computer, a room of one's own for study and so on are costly. Financial resources can also have indirect impacts on the quality of children's environments, for example, poverty leads to stress which may affect parenting (Whitty, 2002; Duncan and Brooks-Gunn, 1997; Mortimore and Whitty, 2000). In addition, the costs and benefits associated with pursuing particular educational options may vary according to the individual's social class of origin (Boudon, 1974; Breen and Goldthorpe, 1997).

Parents' social class and educational qualifications are closely linked, as qualifications are linked to labour market outcomes. Parents' education, and the skills, knowledge, dispositions and practices that go with it, are often described as 'cultural capital'. Bourdieu (1977) states that cultural capital consists of familiarity with the dominant culture in a society, and especially the ability to understand and use 'educated' language. The concept of cultural capital has been interpreted in various ways, but there is a consensus that cultural practices associated with the educated middle-classes, such as reading, are linked to educational attainment (Crook, 1997; Sullivan, 2001; De Graaf et al., 2000).

Social capital inheres in the relationships between people in families, schools and communities. It describes 'features of social organisation, such as trust, norms and networks' (Putnam, 1993) and, with regard to education, it refers to 'the set of resources that inhere in family relations and in community social organisation and that are useful for the cognitive or social development of a child or young person' (Coleman, 1994:300). For Coleman (1988), social capital in the family consists of the physical presence and attention given to the child by family members. Social capital within the school consists of social networks which allow social norms to be established and enforced. Social capital affects parents' relationship with the school, and students' relationships with one another and with their teachers. It is clear that peer group norms impose strong pressures on school students. Power *et al.* (1998) found that, whereas academically-able pupils at a grammar school were likely to worry about not being able to keep up with the work, academically able pupils at a comprehensive were much more likely to worry about other pupils thinking they were too clever. There have also been concerns that boys sanction each other particularly severely for pursuing academic success (Epstein, 1998; Power *et al.*, 1998). Sewell (1997) suggests that exaggerated masculine peer group norms are particularly damaging for African-Caribbean boys. These examples illustrate the complex interactions between class, gender and ethnicity and social capital, and the fact that social capital can have positive or negative consequences for educational attainment. Commitment to education can be strong in certain less affluent groups, and thereby help to counteract material disadvantage to some extent. On the other hand, many working class and minority ethnic students attend schools where links between parents and teachers are weak, or where social norms in the peer group make studying more difficult. Furthermore, differences in social capital have implications for social inclusion as well as educational attainment, as strong 'bonding' capital within one social group may militate against the development of 'bridging' capital across social groups (Putnam, 1995).

Gender

The gender gap at GCSE has been widely commented on, and it is often assumed that the gap must reflect unfairness to boys. There was a jump in the gender gap in the late 1980s, and, understandably, commentators have assumed that the coursework element of GCSE assessment can explain the increased gender gap. However, the evidence suggests that this is not a valid explanation. The dramatic reduction in the coursework element of GCSE assessment in 1994 did not lead to any reduction in the gender gap in attainment.

Another popular explanation for the gender gap is that school environments have become 'feminised', partly due to the high proportion of women in teaching (especially in primary school teaching), and this is unfair to boys, who suffer from a lack of male role models and from 'feminine' teaching styles. There is a striking lack of any empirical evidence to support the view that boys suffer from being taught by women.

The 'culture of laddishness' explanation suggests that there is a particular problem with working class boys (see Leader, 2000). In fact, there is only a small gender gap at lower levels of attainment, and the gender gap is larger among the middle classes than the working classes (Gorard *et al.*, 2001; Sullivan *et al.*, 2004). Working-class girls typically do more domestic work (including child care and elder care), which can interfere with schoolwork and homework.

It is also worth noting that girls have always outperformed boys in the early years of education, but in the past girls' early advantage was not carried through strongly to GCSE level – probably because the view that women's paid work outside the home was not as important as that of men was still prevalent. Since the 1970s, women's labour market participation has increased enormously, family structures have changed, and attitudes to girls' education have changed correspondingly. The trend towards smaller families may also have been particularly beneficial for girls, as parents with limited resources tend to favour sons and often allocate domestic duties to girls. Given these socio-economic changes, it would be surprising if girls' academic attainment had not increased by more than that of boys.

Women's labour market disadvantage persists despite girls' much vaunted triumph over boys at GCSE. Women's under-representation in 'masculine' subject areas such as maths, science, engineering and technology contributes to this problem, although women do not achieve the same occupational status as their male peers even when they have the same qualifications. However, the gap between male and female graduates is far smaller than the gender gap for poorly qualified young school-leavers, as the labour market is far more 'gendered' at the lower-skilled end of the occupational distribution (Power et al., 2003). Young women leaving school with no qualifications are particularly disadvantaged compared to their male peers, as unqualified girls have fewer labour market opportunities open to them than unqualified boys do, and vocational training remains strongly segregated by gender (Bynner et al., 1997; Rake, 2000; Hakim, 1996; Power et al., 2003). For young women, not being in education, employment or training is associated with lone parenthood and depression (Bynner and Parsons, 2002). The fact that unqualified women are more disadvantaged than unqualified men may give girls a greater incentive to achieve at school.

'Race' and ethnicity

There was a consensus in the research literature until the 1980s that minority students 'underachieved' in education (Tomlinson, 1991). This consensus was partly due to the fact that first generation immigrant children, especially those who did not speak English, suffered particular disadvantages. However, methodological crudity in early studies also led to an exaggeration and over-simplification of 'ethnic disadvantage'.

The Swann report (1981), an inquiry into the 'causes of underachievement' of African-Caribbean children, found that these pupils achieved fewer exam passes than white or Asian children. The report was widely criticised for failing to present adequate statistical evidence to assess minority ethnic attainment (Plewis, 1988). 'Asian' pupils were lumped together as an undifferentiated group, and social class and gender differences did not form part of the analyses. More recent research on ethnicity and education has been more sophisticated, yet the picture we have regarding the educational attainment of young people from different ethnic groups is still patchy.

Some studies are limited geographically, while some do not distinguish adequately between ethnic groups with very different national, cultural and socio-economic origins. There is a trade off between using nationally representative data and using data with sufficient representation of ethnic minorities. It is obviously crucial to control for social class in order to isolate specifically ethnic differences, since different ethnic groups have different social class profiles (Drew and Demack, 1998). Family size and family structure have also been neglected, despite the fact that these have long been established as significant predictors of educational outcomes, and ethnic variation in family structure and size has been documented (Modood *et al.*, 1997). Nevertheless, studies that control for social class (Drew and Gray, 1990; Drew, 1995; Haque and Bell, 2001) suggest that ethnic differences in GCSE results are largely explained by this variable, though some minority ethnic students, notably Indians, perform significantly better than whites even when social class is controlled. The evidence regarding participation rates in post-compulsory education suggests that ethnic minorities persist in further and higher education to a greater extent than whites. Drew (1995) finds that Asians are the most likely to stay on in further education, followed by African-Caribbeans, with whites being the least likely to stay on, despite their relatively privileged social class profile.

Even if significant differences between ethnic groups could be robustly established, more fine-grained research would be needed to explore how far these reflect more subtle social intra-class distinctions, economically, socially or culturally, and how far they derive from the effects of racism within communities and schools. In order to inform policy on these matters, we need much better theory as well as data on the relative influence of school, family and community on ethnic differentials in educational attainment. Clearly, outcomes are the result of complex interaction between these different factors. Ethnographic research has focussed strongly on racism within schools. Considerable attention has been given to the way in which schools can discriminate against minority ethnic groups, either through direct racism, or through processes which are indirectly discriminatory. For example, Gillborn and Youdell (2000) and Troyna (1992) describe the way in which school practices such as setting by ability and tiered entry to GCSE can discriminate against minority ethnic groups. Racism and discrimination within schools are clearly extremely important in their own right, yet it is very difficult to say how much impact these factors may have in determining educational outcomes for minority ethnic groups.

Differences in the level of social capital between ethnic groups have been more extensively explored in the US and elsewhere than in Britain. Explanations of unequal educational attainments that refer to the cultural and social characteristics of minority groups have often been viewed with understandable suspicion, as such arguments are seen as 'blaming the victim' (Vermeulen, 2000). Yet economic, social and cultural differences can affect the relationship of children and their families to schooling, sometimes in unexpected ways. Economic disadvantages may be counter-balanced by high levels of social capital within the home and community (Lauglo, 2000), so it is possible for economically disadvantaged minority ethnic communities to promote educational success (Portes and Rumbaut, 2001; Gibson, 2000).

Controlling for educational qualifications, ethnic minorities do not achieve labour market positions and incomes on a par with whites, and face an increased risk of unemployment (Heath and McMahon, 1997; Connor et al., 1996; Heath and Smith, 2003). A likely explanation for the fact that members of minority ethnic groups tend to stay on in further and higher education for longer than similarly qualified whites is that the former anticipate labour market discrimination, and realise that they will need to outperform the white majority in terms of qualifications in order to compete for jobs. A lack of immediate job opportunities may also remove the incentive for minority ethnic youths to quit education (Rivkin, 1995; Leslie and Drinkwater, 1999).

Schooling

It is well established that 'home background' is a much stronger predictor of educational outcomes for children than school attended, but this does not mean that schooling does not matter. On the other hand, the potential role of individual schools in challenging social disadvantage has some-times been exaggerated by policy makers (Mortimore and Whitty 2000).

Researchers in the field of school effectiveness have argued that there are important differences in performance between schools, controlling for student inputs (Rutter et al., 1979; Mortimore et al., 1988; Smith and Tomlinson, 1989; Tizard et al., 1988; Sammons et al., 1995b). However, there are serious methodological difficulties inherent in carrying out school effectiveness research, and these are often underplayed (Goldstein and Woodhouse, 2000). Attempting to control adequately for parental choice of school is a crucial difficulty that faces all such studies (Heath and Clifford, 1981). This challenge remains even when a range of social back-ground measures have been controlled.

Researchers have identified factors that are associated with effective schooling, such as high aspirations and an academic ethos (Schveers and Creemers, 1989; Sammons et al., 1995a). But noting the importance of these characteristics is easier than creating them. Given the importance of social capital, it is likely to be easier to promote characteristics such as high aspirations in some schools and communities than in others (Lupton, 2004).

Clearly, certain school characteristics matter more for some students than for others. For example, there is a consensus in the literature on class sizes that substantial cuts in class size can make a difference for the youngest children, especially for those from disadvantaged backgrounds, and those with low levels of prior attainment (Yang *et al.*, 2000; Blatchford *et al.*, 2002; Prais, 1996). These differential effects are salient in policy terms, as a small cut in class sizes across the board may have no impact, whereas a targeted cut in class sizes could achieve significant effects. In view of recent evidence on the lack of impact of class size on the attainment of older children (Blatchford *et al.*, 2004), the 1997 pledge to lower all infant classes to thirty or fewer pupils was appropriate in terms of age-range but may have been misguided as a way of tackling disadvantage. It benefited suburban rather than inner-city constituencies as, due to falling rolls, inner city schools already had few classes of over thirty children.

There is a consensus that 'teacher effects' matter more than 'school effects', so that, for any given subject, it matters more which class one is in than which school (Scheerens and Bosker, 1997; Teddlie and Reynolds, 2000). Yet only a minority of studies focus on the level of the classroom and the teacher rather than the school as a whole. There is a lack of British research on teacher characteristics, but evidence from the US suggests that teachers' assessed verbal abilities (Ehrenberg and Brewer, 1995), and the selectiveness of the institution where teachers obtained their degree (Ehrenberg and Brewer, 1994) have an effect on students' performance. Rowan *et al.* (1997) show that maths teachers' knowledge of mathematics is positively associated with students' mathematics progress. So, while academic ability is far from being the only important characteristic of good teachers, it does matter. In particular, adequate subject knowledge is not a sufficient condition of good teaching, but it is surely a necessary one. The supply of teachers in Britain has fallen, as teachers' relative pay and status have declined substantially since the 1970s (although teachers' pay has risen since 1997), and there have been particular shortages of teachers with qualifications in maths and science (Chevalier *et al.*, 2002). There was a considerable decline in the relative academic ability of men (but not women) entering teaching in Britain between the late 1970s and the early 1990s (Nickell and Quintini, 2002).

Given this context, schools in disadvantaged areas are unlikely to be able to attract their fair share of good teachers. There is a lack of information on the distribution of teachers according to their qualifications and experience, and Ofsted reports do not detail this type of information, despite its importance for school effectiveness (Bartlett, 2004). However, research shows that teachers in private and selective schools are considerably better qualified than comprehensive school staff (Smithers and Tracey, 2003). Given the difficult working conditions faced by teachers in disadvantaged schools, it would be necessary to increase teacher salaries in these schools or offer other incentives in order to attract sufficient high quality teachers to work in them (Brighouse, 2003).

Government policies

Choice and diversity

For those who can afford it, 'school choice' has always been provided by the private sector. Because Britain incorporated most denominational schools within the state sector, its private sector is relatively small. Throughout the last century, only five to eight per cent of the school aged population has attended private schools (Smith, 2000). British private schools are socially and (often) academically exclusive institutions and the domination of elite occupations by alumni of the top private schools (or 'public schools') has long been apparent (Boyd, 1973). As a result, the existence of private schools has been seen as socially divisive and damaging, and as being closely bound up with British class divisions. Private schools can be seen as creaming off the most privileged children, and the effect of this on state schools is a particular concern in affluent cities, including London, where the proportion of children in private schools is far higher than the national average. Private schools also have a disproportionate share of the students taking A-levels, and regularly top academic league tables. However, research on the role of private schools during the tripartite era suggests that the success of these schools was largely due to their academically and socially privileged intake of students (Feinstein and Symons, 1999; Sullivan and Heath, 2003).

The government's attitude towards the private sector has been somewhat ambivalent. The abolition of the Assisted Places Scheme was a policy designed to appeal to Labour's grass roots, and the government has also criticised the domination of elite universities by private school students. On the other hand, the introduction of 'quasi-markets' to state education provision by the Conservatives was predicated on the view that the introduction of some of the 'disciplines' of the private sector will help to raise standards and the current government has continued the promotion of diversity of educational provision and parental choice of schools. This policy has led to concern that schools may become less academically, socially and ethnically mixed. The possibility of social polarisation is worrying, not only because social mixing between children of different social classes and ethnic groups is worthwhile in itself, but also because school composition has an impact on educational attainment. There is a consensus that this impact is important and that schools with a high proportion of students of low social status or low prior academic ability are at a disadvantage. For example, Levacic and Woods (2002b, 2002a) find the concentration of social disadvantage in a school relative to other local schools has a strong impact on GCSE improvement over time. These effects may be due to the influence of peer groups on aspirations and behaviour, or they may be due to other processes, such as schools with low proportions of 'able' students finding it hard to attract good teachers.

In the education market, certain categories of student are more valuable than others. Schools are keen to attract 'able' and middle class students, and girls (especially those from higher achieving minority ethnic groups) have also come to be seen as an asset (Ball and Gewirtz, 1997). Less popular schools can become male-dominated, as parents demand single-sex schooling for girls more often than for boys. Researchers have documented the way middle class parents marshal a host of resources to get their children into their preferred schools. Money, cultural capital, social capital, and sheer pushiness are all relevant (Carroll and Walford, 1997; Gewirtz et al., 1995; Glatter et al., 1997; West et al., 1991; Woods et al., 1998; Ball, 2003). Studies have suggested that this leads to greater social segregation and polarisation within the school system (Whitty et al., 1998).

But has increased parental choice of school in the UK actually led to more or less polarisation between schools compared to the previous system based on stricter catchment areas and 'selection by mortgage'? (Gorard and Fitz, 2000). Gorard and his colleagues (Gorard et al., 2003; Gorard and Fitz, 2000; Gorard, 2003) have carried out research into school segregation in England and Wales from 1989-2001, focusing on the spread of children eligible for Free School Meals (FSM). Their 'Index of Segregation' is defined as the proportion of students who would have to change schools for there to be an even spread of disadvantage between schools within an area of analysis. For England and Wales, segregation by FSM declined from thirty-five per cent in 1989 to thirty per cent in 1995, but rose to thirty-three per cent between 1997 and 2001. Segregation by ethnicity, SEN, and English as an additional language declined throughout the period. However, social segregation was greater in areas which contained selective schools.

These findings have been controversial (Gibson and Asthana, 2000, 2002; Noden, 2000, 2002; Gorard, 2000, 2002). Much of the criticism levelled at Gorard et al. seems to be based on the view that they claim a causal link between decreased segregation and the introduction of the quasi-market. However, Gorard et al. acknowledge that their research cannot isolate the effect of marketisation, and argue that the level of social segregation is driven largely by social and demographic factors. Several authors have pointed out the crudity of FSM as a measure of socio-economic status (Gorard et al., 2003; Goldstein and Noden, 2003; Brighouse, 2003). A related concern is raised by the possibility that officially 'non-selective' schools, including faith and specialist schools, in fact attract, or even covertly select, particular social groups. Indeed, many critics of New Labour's adoption of the Conservative diversity and choice agenda fear that the mix of specialist schools, faith schools, academies etc. will recreate the tri-partite system, both academically and socially.

Furthermore, the government's encouragement of faith schools relies on some assumptions about their academic performance that still need to be tested. Observers of Catholic schools in the US (Coleman *et al.*, 1982); (Bryk *et al.*, 1993) and in Britain (Grace, 2002) suggest that the relative success of these institutions, particularly with some minority ethnic and disadvantaged groups, may be dependent upon strong levels of social capital within such schools and the communities that they serve. Although at least part of their relative success can be attributed to differences in the academic quality of their intakes, or different patterns of exclusion and differences in academic programmes on offer, there may still be a residual effect of 'community', both in-school and beyond school. If, however, that is the product of the strong 'bonding' (within community) capital in such schools rather than 'bridging' (cross community) capital (Putnam, 1995), this potentially creates a tension between the government's standards agenda and its inclusion agenda. We therefore urgently need to explore how positive forms of social capital can be developed in multi-ethnic and multi/non-denominational schools serving diverse populations.

Much is again made of the apparent capacity of specialist schools to outperform other secondary schools in terms of their examination performance. Recent Key Stage 4 results show specialist schools as not only performing relatively better than supposedly comparable non-specialist schools, but also performing relatively better in official value-added terms (Jesson and Taylor, 2001; Smith, 2004). This evidence is highly contentious and has rarely been subjected to adequate peer review in advance (Schagen and Goldstein, 2002). More rigorous research studies are needed to determine the validity of the claims on either side and assess the impact of specialism, selection and resources on the relative performance of specialist and other schools (Edwards and Tomlinson, 2002).

In the context of the national curriculum, having a curriculum specialism may not in itself differentiate schools significantly. The far more serious threat to the comprehensive ideal comes from the effect that the extra resources and the cachet of the specialist school label may have on recruitment. The early evidence on FSM eligibility in specialist schools suggested that the intakes of such schools might well be socially unrepresentative, though this may be more associated with prior school type than with specialism per se (Gorard and Taylor, 2001). Others have claimed that, as the proportion of such schools increases – potentially now to a hundred per cent – this phenomenon is decreasing (Taylor, 2001).

Given that diversity in secondary education will doubtless remain in place for the foreseeable future, what is crucial is to prevent legitimate differences from becoming unjustifiable inequalities and to stop particular social groups monopolising particular sorts of schools. However, as there is evidence that segregation effects increase where larger numbers of schools are their own admissions authorities (Goldstein and Noden, 2003), this would require greater standardisation of admissions criteria and monitoring of their application, moving well beyond the recently introduced coordinated admissions schemes.

Raising standards and educational expansion

Labour has extended the national curriculum, introducing national literacy and numeracy strategies, now subsumed in an overall primary strategy, and a Key Stage 3 strategy that will soon become part of a wider secondary strategy. The 'Key Stage' testing introduced by the 1988 Education Act has been extended. Schools have been asked to meet ambitious targets for improved performance at each Key Stage. The combination of testing and league tables is designed to give schools an incentive to improve their performance. A key aim is to deal with Britain's 'long tail' of low achievement by raising standards at the bottom end of the distribution.

The publication of league tables of school results has formed a key part of the government's drive to raise standards. 'Value added' tables have been introduced in order to reflect the fact that schools' intakes differ in terms of their prior attainments. The problems associated with 'value added' tables have been discussed extensively by Goldstein, and in a Statistics Commission report (2004)[1]. A fundamental problem with the value added scores is that they control only for pupil attainment at the previous Key Stage, and there are no controls for socio-economic background. Therefore value added scores should not be seen as a measure of school performance, yet they have been presented by DfES as showing 'those schools that perform better than other schools in similar circumstances' (Phipps, 2003).

Government has claimed that the numeracy and literacy strategies have been highly successful in raising standards. However, it is actually rather difficult to assess what impact these strategies have had. Bartlett (2004) has pointed out that, while the percentage of students achieving level 4 in Key Stage 2 English exams increased by ten percentage points between 1998 (when the National Literacy Strategy was introduced) and 2000, there had been an increase of eight percentage points in the two years preceding the introduction of NLS. If things were already improving before the introduction of NLS, we cannot be confident that NLS caused the improvement between 1998 and 2000. The data is consistent with the view that the introduction of testing in itself was instrumental in raising standards, independent of the NLS. The claim that improvements in maths test scores are due to the introduction of the National Numeracy Strategy is similarly questionable (Goldstein, 2003).

Nevertheless, the combination of Key Stage testing and the publication of schools' KS and examination results has provided a powerful incentive for schools to increase the attainments of their pupils. This is likely to have had a very positive impact on pupils at key borderlines such as the C/D borderline at GCSE. Although there are concerns that pupils who fall below

1 Available at http://www. statscom.org. uk/media_ pdfs/cor- respondence/ letter0187.pdf

this level are not seen as a priority, due to the structure of incentives facing schools (Gillborn and Youdell, 2000), it should not be assumed that this implies that working class and minority ethnic students would benefit from the abolition of externally assessed Key Stage tests and GCSEs. While such tests and examinations can be culturally biased (Mortimore and Whitty, 2000), teachers' own assessments can be affected by responses to the non-academic characteristics of students such as gender, ethnicity, social class, perceived character and physical attractiveness (Dusek and Joseph, 1983; Bennett *et al.*, 1993; Doherty and Hier, 1988).

A particularly important equity gain from the introduction of the National Curriculum has been the increased participation of girls in mathematics and science up to GCSE level, which has allowed girls to demonstrate that they are capable of high achievement in these subjects. The reintroduction of earlier choice, including that being proposed by Tomlinson (2004), could undermine these gains. Without real progress towards parity of esteem for different curricular tracks, early (and relatively uninformed) choice could also disadvantage working class students and some minority ethnic groups, as they would be more likely than others to abandon prestigious options.

At GCSE level, there has been a general trend for social class inequality to reduce over time, as overall attainment levels have increased. For example, as the proportion of middle class students getting at least one good GCSE pass has approached a hundred per cent, the middle class rate of improvement over time has slowed, and working class levels of attainment have caught up (Sullivan *et al.*, 2004). The higher the benchmark of attainment, the higher the level of social class inequality. So, the social class gap in getting eight good GCSE passes is greater than the gap in getting five good passes, which in turn is greater than the gap in getting one good pass. While all ethnic groups have improved their GCSE performance over time, patterns of improvement have varied according to ethnicity. From 1992 to 2000, Youth Cohort Study data show all ethnic minority groups except Pakistanis making more progress than whites.

The expansion of the numbers of students in further and higher education (HE) has continued, and tuition fees have been introduced to fund the expansion of HE. The government's declared aim is to 'widen participation' in HE. However, expansion has been accompanied by increased inequalities between rich and poor individuals (Blanden and Machin, 2004) and between people from poor neighbourhoods and better-off neighbourhoods (Galindo-Rueda *et al.*, 2004). The social class gap has increased in absolute terms and stayed constant in proportionate terms (Sullivan *et al.*, 2004). Increased levels of performance at A level, and increased levels of participation in HE have heightened competition for access to prestigious universities and courses. Higher Education performance indicators[2] show a general pattern for the most academically-selective institutions to be most dominated by middle class students.

2 Published in the **Times Higher Education Supplement** 21.5.04, compiled from HEFCE and HESA figures.

Educational expansion is generally seen as progressive and as providing opportunities for groups of people who were previously excluded from educational participation. However, it is well documented internationally that increased overall rates of educational participation do not necessarily lead to a reduction in the association between social class and educational participation (Shavit and Blossfeld, 1993). The gap between social classes generally increases in the early stages of expansion, as the middle classes are able to take up the new opportunities at a faster rate. As the middle classes approach saturation point, the increase in their rate of participation slows, allowing the working classes to catch up (Boudon, 1974). Nevertheless, we have to acknowledge that a qualification diminishes in value as it becomes near-universal. A qualification that everyone holds has no labour-market value. So reductions in social class differentials in educational attainment that are achieved through overall increases in attainment may not have strong consequences for later social mobility.

Conclusions

We need to recognise the continuing importance of social class as a determinant of educational outcomes. Social class is vastly more important in this respect than either ethnicity or gender, yet policymakers are far happier to talk explicitly about gender and ethnicity, and often exaggerate the importance of gender in particular. Studies which contain no controls for social class often claim that the differences they describe are net of social background, but failing to measure social class won't make it go away. Administrative data-sets such as the National Pupil Database need to include rich measures of social background, rather than just FSM. We cannot come to informed conclusions on issues such as school segregation and school effectiveness without better data. Both researchers and policymakers need to be honest about the limitations of the evidence they are using, and what the research can and cannot show.

It is therefore encouraging that the government's five-year strategy for children and learners begins by highlighting the huge influence of social class on early development in this country. (This is illustrated with a graph based on Feinstein (2003) which shows children from higher social class homes with low test scores at age two overtaking lower social class children starting with high test scores by the time they reach age seven). It is less encouraging that some of the policies for schools advocated later in the strategy document may exacerbate rather than mitigate the effects of social class on educational attainment and participation. There is relevant research evidence on these matters that needs to be weighed carefully rather than dismissed or ignored on the grounds of its inconvenience for policy.

As well as better data on students, we need better data on teachers. Research suggests that differences in effectiveness between teachers are greater than those between schools, yet most school effectiveness research has not considered the implications of the possibility that good teachers are an unequally distributed resource. We agree with Bartlett's (2004) proposal that the government should collect and distribute data on teacher qualifications and experience in a form that permits cross-analysis with student demographics and achievement statistics.

Schools in disadvantaged areas face several major obstacles:

- Pupils arrive at school with lower levels of attainment.

- Pupils do not have the same home resources to support learning that more advantaged children have.

- Social norms within the peer group may be less supportive of learning, and the wider community outside the school may also lack the kind of social capital that supports learning. These factors can lead to disruptive behaviour.

- Schools in disadvantaged areas may lack key resources such as good teaching staff, especially in shortage subject areas.

Given all these factors, it should come as no surprise that having a high proportion of FSM pupils in a school is associated with poor OFSTED scores (Lupton, 2004). We fully acknowledge that it is not acceptable for schools to use a low socio-economic profile as an excuse for low expectations and low standards. Nevertheless, judgements on the effectiveness of schools in disadvantaged areas need to take the obstacles faced by these schools into account. It is not good enough to control for proportion of FSM, and then say that all remaining between-schools differences can be attributed to the school alone. Government policies to raise standards in schools with high proportions of disadvantaged students need to take into account the particular problems faced by these schools, and to provide additional support. For example, Brighouse's (2003) suggestions that teachers need greater incentives to work at disadvantaged schools, and that cuts in class sizes should be focused on disadvantaged children rather than spread across the whole population, deserve serious consideration.

The concentration of disadvantaged children in particular schools will also need to be addressed, as the importance of social and academic mix to both the standards and the inclusion agendas is widely recognised by researchers. There are still too many schools in urban areas which have been colonised by particular social groups either deliberately or by default. The recent recommendations on school admissions from the House of Commons Select Committee (2004) could at least reduce the abuses that exacerbate this effect.

Nevertheless, we need to be realistic about the impact of education policy on social inequalities. Government needs to acknowledge that schools cannot compensate for society. Educational policies alone are never likely to eradicate class inequalities in educational attainment. Policies to reduce inequalities in the distribution of income may have a greater impact on educational inequalities than educational policy can (Robinson, 1997). It should be borne in mind that a reduction in educational inequalities will not automatically lead to more equal social mobility chances. Especially in the cases of ethnic and gender inequalities, inequalities in the labour market need direct attention. Women and minority ethnic groups have made great strides in terms of educational attainment, yet still suffer clear labour market discrimination. An exclusive focus on education policy will not resolve this problem.

Finally, even the focus on social mobility may be questionable as the primary policy aim, since high levels of social mobility can co-exist with extreme inequalities in standards of living which may have equally damaging social consequences.

References

Ball, S.J. (2003) *Class Strategies and the Education Market: The middle classes and social advantage* RoutledgeFalmer, London

Ball, S.J. and Gewirtz, S. (1997) 'Girls in the Education Market: Choice, competition and complexity' *Gender and Education* 9(2):207-222

Bartlett, L (2004) *Policy Remedies for Teacher Shortages in the UK and the USA* The Foreign and Commonwealth Office, London

Bennett, R.E., Gottesman, R.L., Rock, D.A. and Cerullo, F. (1993) 'Influence of behavior perceptions and gender on teachers' judgements of students' academic skill' *Journal of Educational Psychology* 85(2):347-356

Blanden, J. and Machin, S. (2004) 'Educational Inequality and the Expansion of UK Higher Education' *Scottish Journal of Political Economy* 51(2):230-249

Blatchford, P., Bassett, P., Brown, P., Martin, C. and Russell, A. (2004) *The Effects of Class Size on Attainment and Classroom Processes in English Primary Schools (Years 4 to 6) 2000-2003* DfES Research Brief RBX13-04

Blatchford, P., Goldstein, H., Martin, C. and Browne, W. (2002) 'A Study of Class Size Effects in English School Reception Year Classes' *British Educational Research Journal* 28(2):169-185

Boudon, R. (1974) *Education, Opportunity and Social Inequality* Wiley, New York.

Bourdieu, P. (1977) 'Cultural Reproduction and Social Reproduction' in Karabel, J. and Halsey, A.H. (eds.) *Power and Ideology in Education* OUP, Oxford

Boyd, D. (1973) *Elites and their Education* NFER, Slough

Breen, R. and Goldthorpe, J. (1997) 'Explaining Educational Differentials: Towards a rational action theory' Rationality and Society 9(3):275-305

Brighouse, H. (2003) 'Learning by example?' *New Economy* 10(4) 230-233

Bryk, A.S., Lee, V.E. and Holland, P.B. (1993) *Catholic Schools and the Common Good* Harvard University Press, Cambridge, Mass

Bynner, J., Morphy, L. and Parsons, S. (1997) 'Women, Employment and Skills' in Metcalf, H. (ed.) *Women and Skills* Policy Studies Institute, London

Bynner, J. and Parsons, S. (2002) 'Social exclusion and the transition from school to work: the case of young people not in education, employment or training' *NEET Journal of Vocational Behaviour* 60:289-309

Carroll, S. and Walford, G. (1997) 'Parents' responses to the school quasi-market' *Research Papers in Education* 12:3-26

Chevalier, A., Dolton, P. and McIntosh, S. (2002) *Recruiting and retaining teachers in the UK: An analysis of graduate occupation choice from the 1960s to the 1990s* Centre for the Economics of Education, LSE, London

Coe, R. and FitzGibbon, C.T. (1998) 'School Effectiveness Research: Criticisms and recommendations' *Oxford Review of Education* 24:421-438

Coleman, J.S. (1988) 'Social Capital in the Creation of Human Capital' *American Journal of Sociology* 94:S94-S120

Coleman, J.S. (1994) *Foundations of Social Theory* Belknap Press, Cambridge, Mass

Coleman, J.S., Hoffer, T. and Kilgore, S. (1982) *High School Achievement: Public, Catholic and private schools compared* Basic Books

Connor, H., LaValle, I., Yackey, N.D. and Perryman, S. (1996) 'Ethnic Minority Graduates: Differences by degree' *Labour Market Trends* 104:395-396

Crook, C.J. (1997) *Cultural Practices and Socioeconomic Attainment: The Australian experience* Greenwood Press, Westport, Connecticut

De Graaf, N.D., De Graaf, P.M. and Kraaykamp, G. (2000) 'Parental Cultural Capital and Educational Attainment in the Netherlands: A refinement of the cultural capital perspective' *Sociology of Education* 73:92-111

Demack, D., Drew, D. and Grimsley, M. (2000) 'Minding the Gap: Ethnic, gender and social class differences in attainment at 16, 1988-95' *Race Ethnicity and Education* 3(2):117-143

DfES (2004) *Statistics of Education: Variation in Pupil Progress 2003*

Doherty, J. and Hier, B. (1988) 'Teacher expectations and specific judgements – a small scale study of the effects of certain non-cognitive variables on teachers' academic predictions' *Educational Review* 40(3):333-348

Douglas, J.W.B. (1964) *The Home and the School* MacGibbon and Kee, London.

Drew, D. (1995) *Race, Education and Work: The statistics of inequality* Avebury, Aldershot

Drew, D. and Demack, D. (1998) 'A League Apart: Statistics in the study of 'race' and education' in Connolly, B. and Troyna, B. (eds.) *Researching Racism in Education: Politics, theory and practice* Open University Press, Buckingham

Drew, D. and Gray, J. (1990) 'The Fifth Year Examination Results of Black Young People in England and Wales' *Educational Research* 32(2):107-117

Duncan, G.J. and Brooks-Gunn, J. (Eds.) (1997) *Consequences of Growing Up Poor* Russell Sage, New York

Dusek, J.D. and Joseph, G. (1983) 'The Bases of Teacher Expectancies: A meta-analysis' *Journal of Educational Psychology* 75(3):327-346

Edwards, T. and Tomlinson, S. (2002) *Selection Isn't Working* The Catalyst Forum, London

Ehrenberg, R.G. and Brewer, D.J. (1994) 'Do School and Teacher Characteristics Matter? Evidence from high school and beyond' *Economics of Education Review* 13(1):1-17

Ehrenberg, R.G. and Brewer, D.J. (1995) 'Did Teachers' Verbal Ability and Race Matter in the 1960s? Coleman revisited' *Economics of Education Review* 14(1):1-21

Epstein, D. (1998) 'Real Boys Don't Work: "Underachievement", masculinity, and the harassment of "sissies"' in Epstein, D., Elwood, J., Hey, V. and Maw, J. (eds.) *Failing Boys Issues in Gender and Achievement* Open University Press, Buckingham, pp. 96-108

Feinstein, L. (2003) 'Inequality in the Early Cognitive Development of British Children in the 1970 Cohort' *Economica* 70(1):73-97

Feinstein, L. and Symons, J. (1999) 'Attainment in Secondary School' *Oxford Economic Papers* 51:300-321

Fogelman, K.R. (ed.) (1983) *Growing up in Great Britain* Macmillan, London

Fogelman, K.R. and Goldstein, H. (1976) 'Social Factors Associated with Changes in Educational Attainment between 7 and 11 Years of Age' *Educational Studies* 2:95-109

Galindo-Rueda, F., Marcenaro-Gutierrez, O. and Vignoles, A. (2004) *The Widening Socio-economic Gap in UK Higher Education* Centre for the Economics of Education

Gewirtz, S., Ball, S.J. and Bowe, R. (1995) *Markets, Choice and Equity in Education* Open University Press, Buckingham

Gibson, A. and Asthana, S. (2000) 'What's in a number? Commentary on Gorard and Fitz's "Investigating the determinants of segregation between schools"' *Research Papers in Education* 15(2):133-153

Gibson, A. and Asthana, S. (2002) 'Understanding Social Polarisation: A possible research agenda' *Research Papers in Education* 17(4):414-415

Gibson, M. (2000) 'Situational and Structural Rationales for the School Performance of Immigrant Youth: Three cases' in Vermeulen, H. and Perlmann, J. (eds.) *Immigrants, Schooling and Social Mobility* Macmillan, London, pp. 72-102

Gillborn, D. and Mirza, H.S. (2000) *Educational Inequality: Mapping race, class and gender* OFSTED, London

Gillborn, D. and Youdell, D. (2000) *Rationing Education: Policy, practice, reform and equity* Open University Press, Buckingham

Glatter, R., Woods, P.A. and Bagley, C. (eds.) (1997) *Choice and Diversity in Schooling: Perspectives and prospects* Routledge, London

Goldstein, H. (2003)

Goldstein, H. and Noden, P. (2003) 'Modelling Social Segregation' Oxford Review of Education 29(2):225-237

Goldstein, H. and Woodhouse, G. (2000) 'School Effectiveness Research and Education Policy' *Oxford Review of Education* 26:353-363

Gorard, S. (2000) 'Here We Go Again: A reply to "What's in a number?" by Gibson and Asthana' *Research Papers in Education* 15(2):155-162

Gorard, S. (2002) 'The Missing Impact of Marketisation Revisited' *Research Papers in Education* 17(4):412-414

Gorard, S. (2003) 'Integration in an Age of Choice' *New Economy* 10(4):240-244

Gorard, S. and Fitz, J. (2000) 'Investigating the Determinants of Segregation between Schools' *Research Papers in Education* 15(2):115-132

Gorard, S., Rees, G. and Salisbury, J. (2001) 'Investigating the Patterns of Differential Attainment of Boys and Girls at School' *British Educational Research Journal* 27(2):125-139

Gorard, S. and Taylor, C. (2001) 'Specialist Schools in England: Track record and future prospects' Occasional Paper, School of Social Sciences, Cardiff University, 44

Gorard, S., Taylor, C. and Fitz, F. (2003) *Schools, Markets and Choice Policies* RoutledgeFalmer, London.

Grace, G. (2002) *Catholic Schools: Mission, market and morality* RoutledgeFalmer, London.

Hakim, C. (1996) *Key Issues in Women's Work* Athlone, London

Halsey, A.H., Heath, A. and Ridge, J. (1980) *Origins and Destinations* OUP, Oxford

Haque, Z. and Bell, J.F. (2001) 'Evaluating the Performances of Minority Ethnic Pupils in Secondary Schools' *Oxford Review of Education* 27(3):357-368

Heath, A. and Clifford, P. (1981) 'The Measurement and Explanation of School Differences' *Oxford Review of Education* 7:33-40

Heath, A. and McMahon, D. (1997) 'Education and Occupational Attainments: The impact of ethnic origins' in Halsey *et al.* (eds.) *Education: Culture, Economy and Society* OUP, Oxford, pp. 646-662

Heath, A. and Smith, S. (2003) 'Mobility and Ethnic Minorities' *New Economy* 10(4):199-204

Hellevik, O. (1997) 'Class Inequality and Egalitarian Reform' *Acta Sociologica* 40(4):377-398

Ireson, J. and Rushforth, K. (2004) *Mapping the Nature and Extent of Private Tutoring at Transition Points in Education* BERA UMIST Manchester.

Jesson, D. and Taylor, C. (2001) *Educational Outcomes and Value Added Analysis of Specialist Schools for the Year 2000* Technology Colleges Trust, London

Jonsson, J. and Mills, C. (1993a) 'Social Class and Educational Attainment in Historical Perspective: A Swedish English comparison (Part 1)' *British Journal of Sociology* 44(2):213-247

Jonsson, J. and Mills, C. (1993b) 'Social Class and Educational Attainment in Historical Perspective: A Swedish English comparison (Part 2)' *British Journal of Sociology* 44(3):403-428

Lauglo, J. (2000) 'Social Capital Trumping Class and Cultural Capital' in Baron, S. (ed.) *Social Capital: Critical perspectives* OUP, Oxford

Leader (2000) 'The Trouble with Boys' *Guardian* 21.8.00

Leslie, D. and Drinkwater, S. (1999) 'Staying on in Full-time Education: Reasons for high participation among ethnic minority males and females' *Economica* 66:63-77

Levacic, R. and Woods, P.A. (2002a) 'Raising School Performance in the League Tables (Part 1): Disentangling the effects of social disadvantage' *British Educational Research Journal* 28(2):207-226

Levacic, R. and Woods, P.A. (2002b) 'Raising School Performance in the League Tables (Part 2): Barriers to responsiveness in three disadvantaged schools' *British Educational Research Journal* 28(2):227-247

Lupton, R. (2004) *Schools in Disadvantaged Areas: Recognising context and raising quality*

Mortimore, P., Sammons, P., Stoll, L., Lewis, D. and Ecob, R. (1988) *School Matters* Open Books, London

Mortimore, P. and Whitty, G. (2000) *Can School Improvement Overcome the Effects of Disadvantage?* Revised edition, Institute of Education, London

Nickell, S. and Quintini, G. (2002) 'The Consequenses of the Decline in Public Sector Pay in Britain: A little bit of evidence' *The Economic Journal* 112

Noden, P. (2000) 'Rediscovering the Impact of Marketisation: Dimensions of social segregation in England's secondary schools 1994-99' *British Journal of Sociology of Education* 21(3):371-390

Noden, P. (2002) 'Education Markets and Social Polarisation: Back to square one?' *Research Papers in Education* 17(4):409-412

Phipps, C. (2003) 'What the Tables Mean: Claire Phipps explains how the DfES has attempted to highlight better performing schools' *Guardian* 23.1.03

Plewis, I. (1988) 'Assessing and Understanding the Educational Progress of Children from Different Ethnic Groups' *Journal of the Royal Statistical Society* 151:316-326

Portes, A. and Rumbaut, R.G. (2001) *Legacies: The story of the immigrant second generation* University of California Press, Berkeley

Power, S., Edwards, T., Whitty, G. and Wigfall, V. (2003) *Education and the Middle Class* Open University Press, Buckingham

Power, S., Whitty, G., Edwards, T. and Wigfall, V. (1998) 'Schoolboys and Schoolwork: Gender identification and academic achievement' *International Journal of Inclusive Education* 2(2):135-153

Prais, S. (1996) 'Class-size and Learning: The Tennessee experiment – what follows?' *Oxford Review of Education* 22(4):399-414

Putnam, R.D. (1993) *Making Democracy Work: Civic traditions in modern Italy* Princeton University Press, Princeton

Putnam, R.D. (1995) 'Bowling Alone: America's declining social capital' *The Journal of Democracy* 6(1):65-78

Rake, K. (ed.) (2000) *Women's Incomes over the Lifetime* The Cabinet Office, London

Rivkin, S.G. (1995) 'Black-White Differences in Schooling and Employment' *Journal of Human Resources* 30(4):826-852

Robinson, P. (1997) *Literacy, Numeracy and Economic Performance* Centre for Economic Performance, London

Rowan, B., Chiang, F.-S. and Miller, R.J. (1997) 'Using Research on Employees' Performance to Study the Effects of Teachers on Students' Achievement' *Sociology of Education* 70:256-284

Rutter, M., Maughan, B., Mortimore, P. and Janet, O. (1979) *Fifteen Thousand Hours* Open Books, London

Sammons, P., Hillman, J. and Mortimore, P. (1995a) *Key Characteristics of Effective Schools: A review of school effectiveness research* Institute of Education for OFSTED, London

Sammons, P., Nuttall, D., Cuttance, P. and Thomas, S. (1995b) 'Continuity of School Effects: A longitudinal analysis of primary and secondary school effects on GCSE performance' *School Effectiveness and School Improvement* 6(4):285-307

Schagen, I. and Goldstein, H. (2002) 'Do Specialist Schools Add Value? Some methodological problems' *Research Intelligence* 80:12-15

Scheerens, J. and Bosker, R.J. (1997) *The Foundations of Educational Effectiveness* Pergamon, Oxford

Schuller, T., Preston, J., Hammond, C., Brassett-Grundy, A. and Bynner, J. (2004) *The Benefits of Learning: Impact of education on health, family life and social capital* Macmillan, Basingstoke

Schveers, J. and Creemers, B.P.M. (1989) 'Conceptualising School Effectiveness' *International Journal of Education Research* 13

Sewell, T. (1997) *Black Masculinities and Schooling* Trentham Books, Stoke-on-Trent

Shavit, Y. and Blossfeld, H.P. (eds.) (1993) *Persistent Inequality: Changing educational attainment in thirteen countries* Westview Press, Boulder

Smith, D. and Tomlinson, S. (1989) *The School Effect: A study of multi-racial comprehensives* Policy Studies Institute, London

Smith, G. (2000) 'Schools' in Halsey, A. H. and Webb, J. (eds.) *Twentieth Century British Social Trends* Macmillan, London

Smith, N. (2004) 'Specialists' Delight as They Trounce Rest' *Times Educational Supplement* 16.1.04

Smithers, A. and Tracey, L. (2003) *Teacher Qualifications* The Sutton Trust, Centre for Education and Employment Research.

Sullivan, A. (2001) 'Cultural Capital and Educational Attainment' *Sociology* 35(4):893-912

Sullivan, A. and Heath, A. (2003) Intakes and Examination Results at State and Private Schools in Walford, G. (ed.) *British Private Schools: Research on policy and practice* Woburn Press, London, pp. 77-104

Sullivan, A., Heath, A. and Rothon, C. (2004) 'Educational Expansion and Social Class Differentials' draft

Taylor, C. (2001) 'Specialist Schools – The real facts behind their success' *Technology Colleges Trust News* 18

Teddlie, C. and Reynolds, D. (2000) *The International Handbook of School Effectiveness Research* Falmer Press, London

Tizard, B., Blatchford, P., Burke, J., Farquhar, C. and Plewis, I. (1988) *Young Children at School in the Inner City* Lawrence Erlbaum Associates, Hove

Tomlinson, S. (1991) 'Ethnicity and Educational Attainment in England – An overview' *Anthropology and Education Quarterly* 22(2):121-139

Troyna, B. (1992) 'Ethnicity and the Organisation of Learning Groups – A Case Study' *Educational Research* 34(1):45-55

Vermeulen, H. (2000) 'Introduction: The role of culture in explanations of social mobility' in Vermeulen, H. and Perlmann, J. (eds.) *Immigrants, Schooling and Social Mobility* Macmillan, London, pp. 1-21

Ward, L. (2004) 'Pupils at good schools "gain 18 months"' *Guardian* 9.8.04

Weiner, G., Arnot, M. and David, M. (1997) Is the Future Female? in Halsey, A. H., Lauder, H., Brown, P. and Wells, A. S. (eds.) *Education: Culture, economy and society* Oxford University Press

West, A., Vaarlaam, A. and Scott, G. (1991) 'Choosing a Secondary School' *Educational Research* 33(1):22-30

Whitty, G. (2002) *Making Sense of Education Policy* Paul Chapman, London

Whitty, G., Power, S. and Halpin, D. (1998) *Devolution and Choice in Education: The school, the state and the market* Open University Press, Buckingham

Woods, P.A., Bagley, C. and Glatter, R. (1998) *School Choice and Competition: Markets in the public interest?* Routledge, London

Yang, M., Goldstein, H., Omar, R., Turner, R. and Thompson, S.G. (2000) 'Meta analysis using multilevel models with an application to the study of class size effects' *Journal of the Royal Statistical Society, Series C* 49:1-14

5 Understanding recent trends in income inequality

Alissa Goodman, Jonathan Shaw and Andrew Shephard

1 Much of the paper is based on analysis undertaken for 'Inequality and Poverty in Britain, 2004' by Mike Brewer, Alissa Goodman, Michal Myck, Jonathan Shaw, and Andrew Shephard (IFS Commentary No. 96 http://www. ifs.org.uk/ inequality/

2 The results we present for years prior to 1994-5 are derived from the Family Expenditure Survey (FES), a sample of 7,000–8,000 households. comm96.pdf), for which Financial support from the Nuffield Foundation ('Inequality in the 1990s', grant number OPD/00111/G) and from the ESRC-funded Centre for the Micro- economic Analysis of Public Policy at IFS (grant number M535255111) is grate- fully acknowl- edged.

Since the mid–1990s, Britain has experienced an unusual combination of slightly rising income inequality and falling relative poverty. This paper sets out the main changes in the income distribution making this combination come about, and discusses some of the drivers of these trends, including changes in the underlying distribution of income, employment changes, and tax and benefit changes.[1]

All the figures in this Note rely on household income data derived from the latest official Households Below Average Income (HBAI) statistics (Department for Work and Pensions, 2004). These tell us about the extent of income inequality in Great Britain up to and including the financial year 2002–3.

Most of the analysis uses weekly household income from all sources, including benefits and net of direct taxes (income tax, National Insurance and council tax) as a measure of living standards. In order to understand the drivers of change, we also consider a measure of gross income, mea- sured before benefits and tax credits are received, and before direct taxes have been paid. All incomes are calculated using information collected from the annual Family Resources Survey (FRS), a representative survey of around 45,000 people in 25,000 households in Great Britain.[2] In all cases we consider incomes before housing costs have been paid for (often referred to as BHC income).

It should also be noted that incomes are measured at the household level, and have been equivalised to take into account family size and composition, using the McClements equivalence scale. All incomes are expressed as the equivalent income for a couple with no dependent chil- dren and in average 2002–3 prices.

Income inequality in Britain: how unequal are we?

There is considerable inequality in the distribution of income in Britain. Figure 5.1 shows a picture of the distribution of income in 2002–3, with the population divided into ten pound bands of net equivalised income. The alternatively shaded light and dark sections represent tenths of the popula- tion, or decile groups. The degree of inequality can be seen from the skewed shape of Figure 5.1. Roughly two thirds of the population have household incomes below the mean, whilst there is a long tail of high incomes – with more than a million individuals above £1,100 per week, the point at which

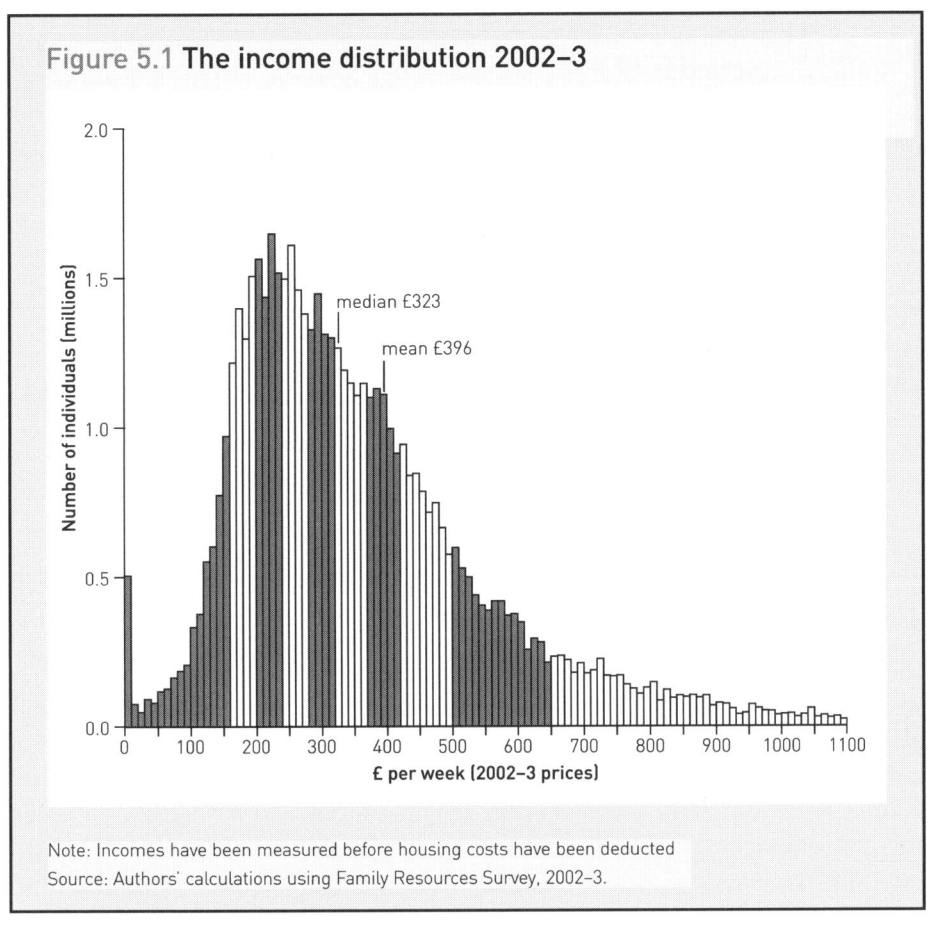

Figure 5.1 **The income distribution 2002–3**

median £323

mean £396

Number of individuals (millions)

£ per week (2002–3 prices)

Note: Incomes have been measured before housing costs have been deducted
Source: Authors' calculations using Family Resources Survey, 2002–3.

this graph has been truncated.

A wide range of indicators can be used to summarise the degree of inequality represented by the above distribution. Table 5.1 shows a number of these, revealing a considerable degree of inequality in after tax, net incomes. In particular, it is interesting to note that the top one per cent of the net income distribution accounts for eight per cent of the total income, a share eight times higher than their population share would suggest, whilst the top ten per cent see almost thirty per cent of the total equivalised, after tax income. Of course these inequality indices are more meaningful when set into context. Below we set out some of the main changes over recent years.

Before proceeding, it is worth noting that we will be adopting a relative notion of inequality in our discussion of income inequality. This means that should all incomes increase or decrease by the same proportional amount, we would conclude that income inequality had remained unchanged. In other words, it is relative, rather than absolute, income differences that we consider here.

Table 5.1 Summary inequality statistics, 2002–3

	Net equivalised income
Share of top 1%	8.0%
Share of top 10%	27.7%
Share of bottom 10%	2.8%
Share of richest 20%/share of poorest 20%[1]	5.6
'90/10' ratio	4.0
'75/25' ratio	2.1
Gini coefficient	0.344

Note: Household incomes have been equivalised and are measured before housing costs have been deducted.

1 See Box 5.1 (p.82) for international comparisons based on this measure.

Source: Authors' calculations using Family Resources Survey 2002–3.

What has happened to income inequality?

Income inequality rose rapidly in this country over the 1980s; subsequently we have returned to a pattern of fluctuating inequality, but the high overall levels of inequality inherited from the 1980s have shown little sign of being reversed. The most commonly used summary measure of inequality is the Gini coefficient. The Gini coefficient is a popular measure of income inequality that condenses the entire income distribution into a single number between zero and one: the higher the number, the greater the degree of income inequality. A value of zero corresponds to the absence of inequality, so that having adjusted for household size and composition, all individuals have the same household income. In contrast, a value of one corresponds to inequality in its most extreme form, with a single individual having command over the entire income in the economy.

The period of the Labour government has been one characterised by slightly rising inequality over the first two years of the first term as measured by the Gini coefficient (see Figure 5.2), and slight falls in inequality over the most recent two years for which we have data. The decreases in inequality over the last year and over the last two years are not statistically significant,[3] but the rise in inequality over the entire period 1996–7 to 2002–3 (from a Gini coefficient of 0.33 to 0.34) is statistically significant at the five per cent level. This means that there is less than a one in twenty chance that inequality has not changed since 1996–7.

While the increase in inequality since 1996–7 is not historically large (for example, between 1979 and 1990, the Gini increased from 0.25 to 0.34), the level certainly is. Indeed, since 1998–9, inequality as measured by the Gini coefficient has been at its highest level since at least 1961.

3 Using the data available to us for this analysis, year-on-year changes in the Gini coefficient are rarely large enough relative to their standard error to be statistically significant. Since 1979, year-on-year changes in the Gini have only been significant at the five per cent level on four occasions: between 1984 and 1985, 1986 and 1987, 1987 and 1988, and 1989 and 1990.

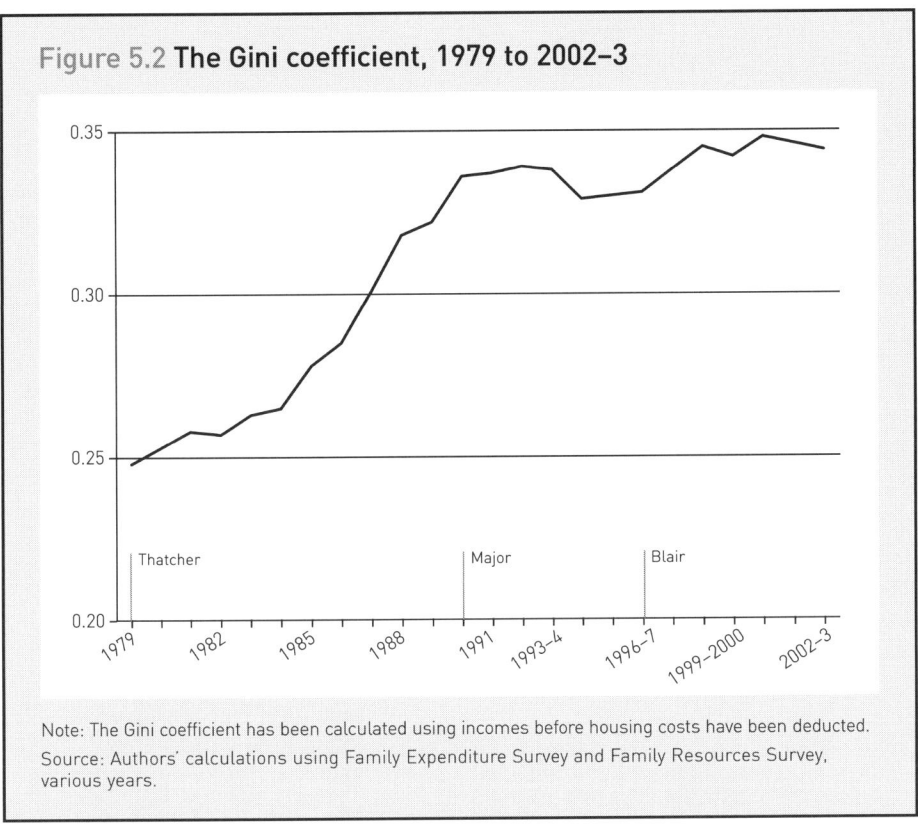

Figure 5.2 **The Gini coefficient, 1979 to 2002–3**

Note: The Gini coefficient has been calculated using incomes before housing costs have been deducted.

Source: Authors' calculations using Family Expenditure Survey and Family Resources Survey, various years.

Meanwhile, Box 5.1 provides some European comparisons of income inequality.

Alternative measures of inequality

The Gini coefficient is only one possible measure of inequality. There are additionally a number of alternative inequality indices, which similarly consider all points in the distribution, which display the same pattern of rising income inequality since 1996–7.[4] However, there are also other popular measures which measure income inequality by comparing incomes at different percentile points in the distribution – for example, at the ninetieth and tenth percentile points (the 90/10 ratio). Figure 5.3 demonstrates that income growth at the tenth and ninetieth percentile points have been of roughly equal magnitudes since 1996–7, and so inequality as measured by the 90/10 ratio remains approximately constant over this period (the income of the individual at the ninetieth percentile point is roughly four times that of the individual located at the tenth percentile point).

If we are genuinely concerned about the accuracy with which the incomes of the poorest and the richest individuals are recorded, then a percentile ratio that does not take into account the richest and poorest individuals may seem desirable as a measure of income inequality. However, the

4 These include the Mehran index, the Piesch index, the Kakwani index, the Theil entropy and mean log deviation indices, and the Atkinson inequality index.

Box 5.1 **European comparisons of income inequality**

The graphs below show levels of inequality in the EU. They show the total income of the richest twenty per cent of individuals expressed as a multiple of the total income of the poorest twenty per cent; the higher is this number, the greater is inequality, with a value of one indicating complete equality. In the UK, for example, the richest twenty per cent of individuals had a total income that was approximately five times that of the poorest twenty per cent. Over the period 1996–2001, inequality on this measure either stayed the same or fell in most countries; the only notable increase occurred in Finland. So even though there has been little change in inequality in the UK over this period, its ranking appears to have deteriorated from sixth-worst to fourth-worst amongst the fifteen EU countries.

European inequality compared, 1996

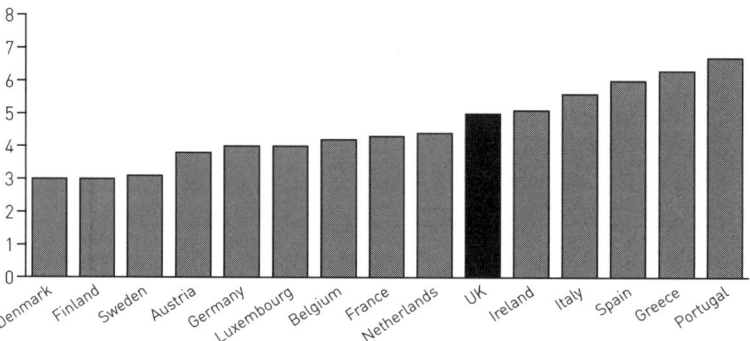

European inequality compared, 2001

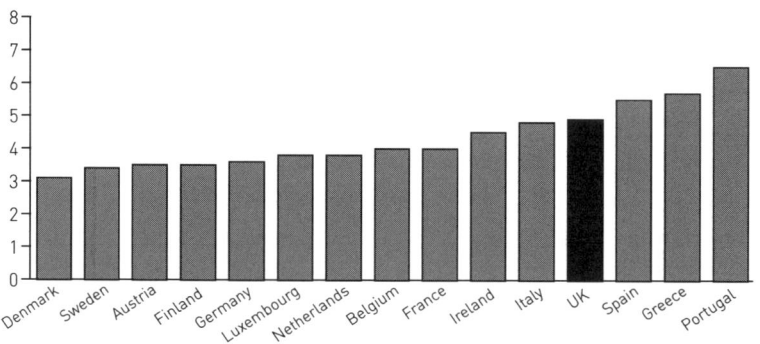

Note: Data for Sweden are for 1997 and 2001.

Source: Eurostat Structural Indicators, table SC010 (europa.eu.int/comm/eurostat/newcronos/queen/public/xml/theme0/strind/socohe-csv.zip).

change in inequality we observe will be sensitive to the choice of percentile points: if we were, for example, to consider the 95/5 ratio, then we would observe an increase in inequality. By contrast, the 75/25 ratio, like the 90/10 ratio has fallen over this time (see Figure 5.2). Furthermore, this measure ignores all the information contained in the middle of the income distribution – one of our motivations for considering the Gini as an inequality measure is that it takes into account all points in the distribution.

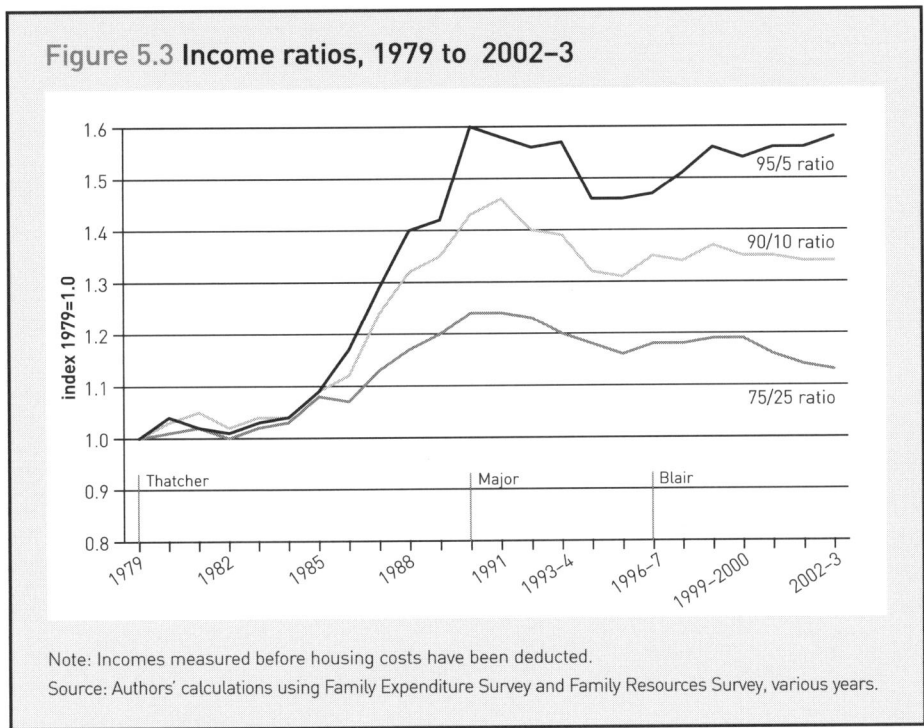

Figure 5.3 **Income ratios, 1979 to 2002–3**

Note: Incomes measured before housing costs have been deducted.
Source: Authors' calculations using Family Expenditure Survey and Family Resources Survey, various years.

The drivers of inequality change

Although the inequality indices shown in Figures 5.2 and 5.3 have shown only small changes in inequality in recent years, such summary statistics mask some important changes to the distribution of incomes, which have been driving these changes.

Rising inequality at the extremes, growing equality in incomes inbetween

First, it is important to note that the slight increase in inequality detected when using inequality measures which capture all points in the distribution has been driven by changes at the very top and very bottom of the distribution: in between if anything, incomes became a little more equal. This point is illustrated by Figure 5.4, which shows how income has grown at ninety-nine percentile points in the income distribution, with the differently shaded sections corresponding to different income decile groups.

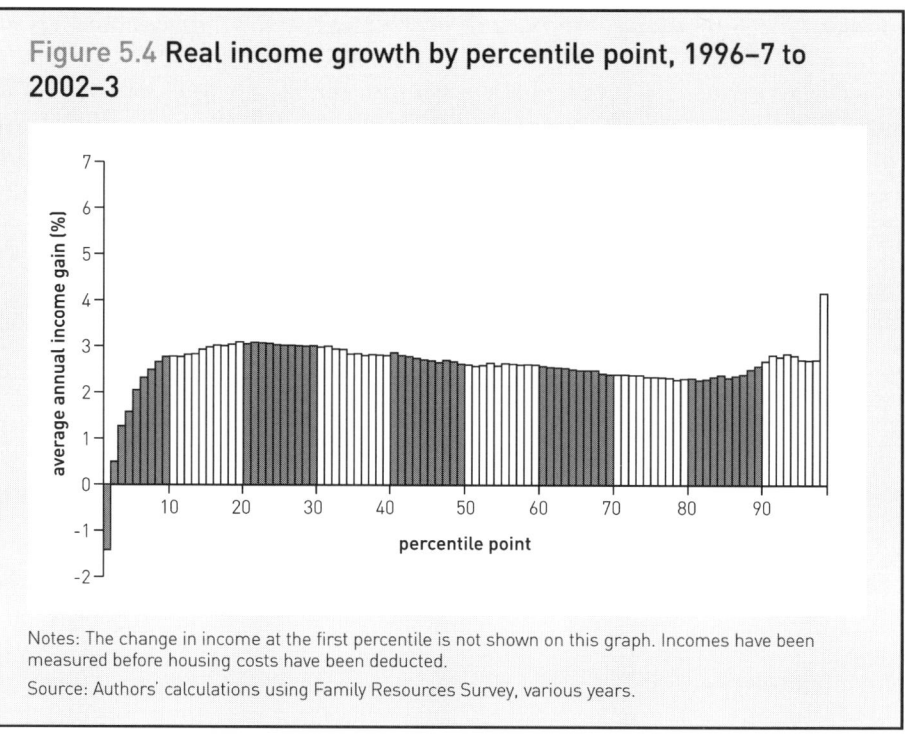

Figure 5.4 **Real income growth by percentile point, 1996–7 to 2002–3**

Notes: The change in income at the first percentile is not shown on this graph. Incomes have been measured before housing costs have been deducted.

Source: Authors' calculations using Family Resources Survey, various years.

This graph gives a much more detailed impression about how the entire distribution of incomes has been changing.

Between about the fifteenth percentile point and the eighty-fifth percentile point, it is generally the poorer individuals who have gained most over the period, and this would be consistent with falling inequality. This is also consistent with the falling rates of relative poverty, particularly amongst families with children that we have seen in recent years (see Brewer *et al.*, 2004). However, it is the behaviour outside of this range that is more dramatic, and the likely cause of the increase in income inequality as measured by the Gini coefficient.

The changes at the very top of the income distribution are quite striking. Beyond the eighty-fifth percentile point, income growth between the two years we have chosen for comparison is generally increasing in income, with a spike at the ninety-ninth percentile point where annual income growth stands at 4.2 per cent – higher than at any other percentile point. This growth in the top one per cent of incomes is confirmed by other recent research examining changes in the incomes of the rich using data from income tax returns (see, for example, Atkinson (2003)). Although we do not know for sure exactly what explains this rapid growth in top incomes – which started during the 1980s and has continued over the 1990s – some possible explanations include changes in the nature of executive remuneration, and the dynamic effects of the cut in top rates of income tax over the

1980s on capital accumulation (see Atkinson (2003) for Britain and Piketty and Saez (2003) for the US).

The changes in incomes amongst the poorest are even less well understood. For individuals below approximately the fifteenth percentile point, income growth since 1996–7 is lower, the poorer is the individual; for the first and second percentile points, the HBAI methodology suggests that growth is actually negative. However, it is difficult to disentangle genuine trends from measurement error in incomes at the very bottom of the distribution. Income levels amongst the bottom one per cent of the income scale, in particular, appear to be especially unstable from year to year, and are most likely very unreliably measured. In addition, we must recall that the annualised income growth rates given at the various percentile points of the income distribution are sample statistics. As such, they have a sampling variance attached, and so even in the absence of any measurement error, it is possible that the 'true' changes could be quite different. This is particularly the case at both extremes of the distribution, where the confidence intervals are quite wide (the wider is the confidence interval, the lower is the precision of the estimate), and in contrast to the richest group of individuals, there does not exist any administrative data for the poorest households against which we can corroborate what we observe in the HBAI data.

However, the fact that income growth has been lowest amongst the bottom fifteen per cent is unlikely to be purely a measurement phenomenon. A number of other explanations are possible. For example, some individuals may not be taking up all the benefits to which they are entitled. This may be because their incomes are only temporarily very low; alternatively, it may be because of more serious take-up issues, as the reach of means-testing has been extended over the period.[5] While it may not necessarily be due to non-take-up, total benefit income accruing to the bottom income decile group has barely risen in real terms over the period in question, averaging about 0.3 per cent a year. By contrast, benefit income growth in the second decile group has been stronger, averaging over two per cent a year. It is clear that more research is required to understand the underlying causes better.

A comparison with the 1980s

It is important to realise that the increase in inequality seen since 1996–7 is very different in nature from that observed over the 1980s, when inequality also increased. Figure 5.2 has already shown the large increase in the Gini coefficient over this period. In Figure 5.5, we now show the real income growth by percentile point under Margaret Thatcher. To aid comparison, a line has been superimposed that shows the associated percentile point growth under Blair as illustrated in Figure 5.4.

Almost without exception, over the period 1979 to 1990, the higher is income, the greater is income growth; if we instead looked at income over

5 Blundell and Preston (1998) offer the first as an explanation for rising income inequality over the 1980s.

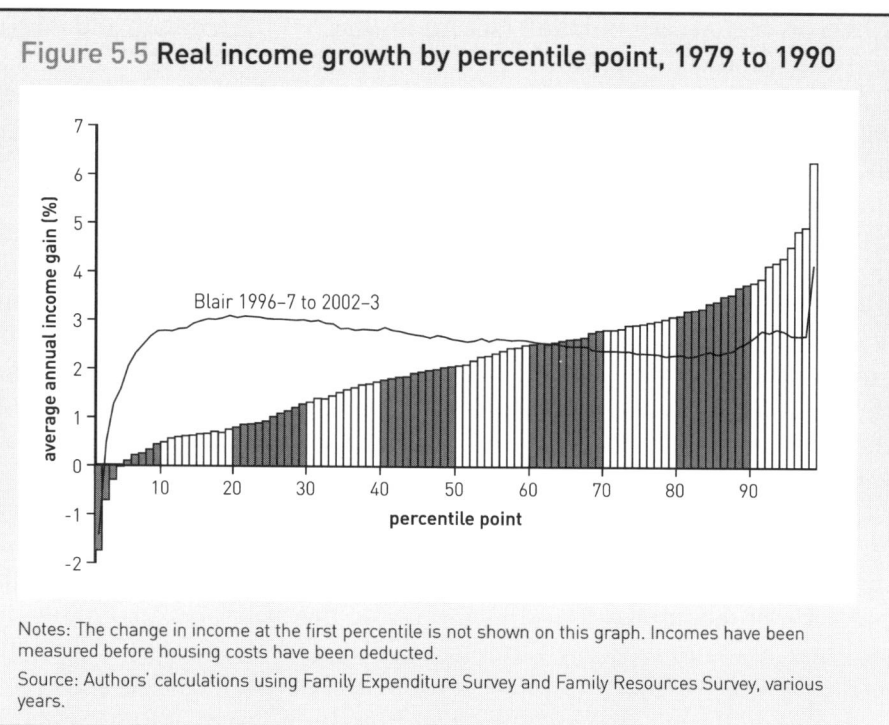

Figure 5.5 Real income growth by percentile point, 1979 to 1990

Blair 1996–7 to 2002–3

(x-axis) percentile point
(y-axis) average annual income gain (%)

Notes: The change in income at the first percentile is not shown on this graph. Incomes have been measured before housing costs have been deducted.

Source: Authors' calculations using Family Expenditure Survey and Family Resources Survey, various years.

6 In calculating these simulated incomes, individuals are awarded all benefits for which they appear eligible and no behavioural responses are allowed for. Because modelled incomes may differ from reported incomes under any observed tax and benefit system, calibration techniques are also applied to the simulated income series.

7 In uprating the tax and benefit system, it is assumed that council tax rises in line with the retail price index. When we instead construct this counterfactual using the observed increases in council tax, we obtain very similar results.

the period from 1984 to 1990, then this pattern would be even more pronounced. Individuals located in the lower decile groups have fared considerably better in recent years than they did in the 1980s. Clearly, therefore, the nature of increasing inequality over the 1980s is very different from that of the increased inequality since 1996–7.

Increasing inequality, yet increasing redistribution

We noted above that in the interval between the fifteenth and eighty-fifth percentiles, incomes became, if anything, somewhat more equal during the period of the Labour Government. An important driver of this has been the effect of government tax and benefit reforms. One way of assessing the contribution of government tax and benefit policies on inequality is to ask how the change in income inequality we have observed compares with what would have happened if the tax and benefit system had remained unchanged.

Since we do not observe the distribution of income under an unchanged tax and benefit system over time, simulation techniques are necessary. Here, we use the IFS tax and benefit model, TAXBEN, to calculate what incomes would have been under an appropriately uprated April 1996 tax and benefit system.[6] From this calculated income series, the Gini coefficient and other inequality measures may be constructed.

In Figure 5.6, we compare the actual Gini coefficient from 1996–7 to 2002–3 and the simulated Gini under the uprated April 1996 tax and benefit system.[7]

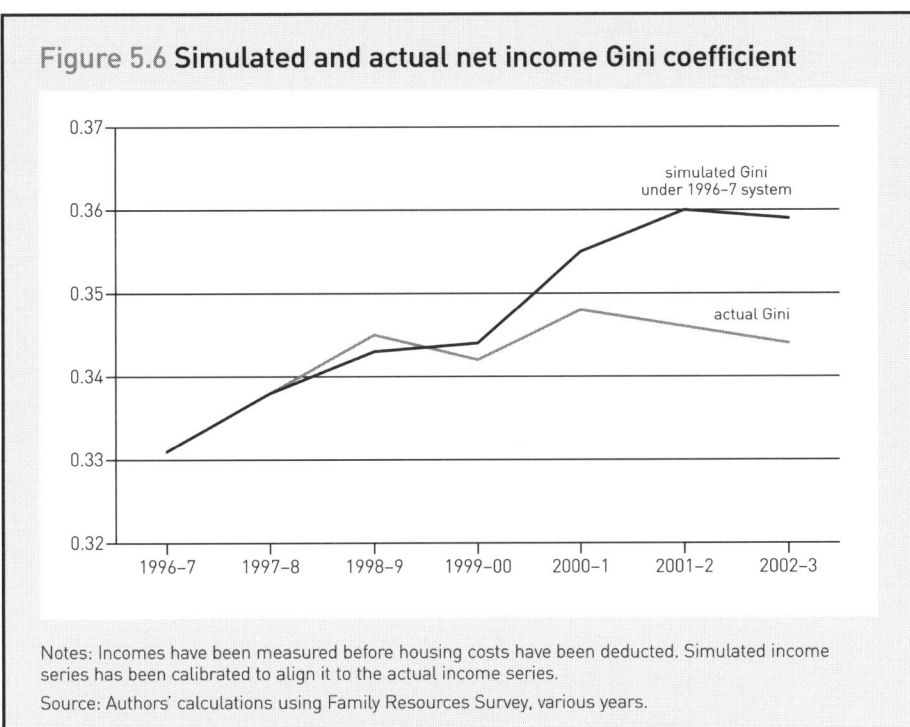

Figure 5.6 **Simulated and actual net income Gini coefficient**

Notes: Incomes have been measured before housing costs have been deducted. Simulated income series has been calibrated to align it to the actual income series.

Source: Authors' calculations using Family Resources Survey, various years.

Our analysis here suggests that from 1996–7 to 1999–2000, the tax and benefit reforms of the Labour government did little to affect inequality compared with what would have been observed if they had simply uprated the April 1996 system.

That the government did little to alter the course of income inequality through changes to personal taxes and benefits in its first few years is not surprising, since Labour's early Budgets contained relatively few redistributive measures affecting incomes before 2000–1.[8] However, since 2000–1, there has been a notable departure between the actual pattern of inequality and the simulated pattern under the April 1996 system.[9] This coincides with the introduction of large increases in means-tested benefits and tax credits, particularly those aimed at families with children and at pensioners (for a summary, see Brewer, Clark and Wakefield (2002)). While the actual level of inequality as measured by the Gini coefficient is similar in 2002–3 to what it was three or four years earlier, the simulations suggest that the Gini coefficient would have increased considerably if the tax and benefit system had remained unchanged.[10]

Our analysis suggests that the redistributive measures of the present government have reduced the increase in inequality that we would otherwise have seen. But it is sobering to note that even the relatively large redistributive programme introduced by Labour since 1997 has only been sufficient to just about halt the growth in inequality, and certainly not to

8 An exception was the introduction of the working families' tax credit from October 1999, although the full effect of this measure would only be reflected in the 2000–1 data.

9 The same pattern emerges when considering incomes on an after-housing-costs basis.

10 Our estimate of inequality if the government had not made any tax and benefit changes has assumed that people's labour market behaviour does not depend on the tax and benefit system. This is, of course, untrue.

reduce it. The orders of magnitude involved are also instructive: the tax and benefit measures introduced under Labour have lowered the growth in the Gini coefficient by around one and a half percentage points; this compares with the total increase in income inequality over the 1980s and 1990s (up to its peak in 2000–1) of around ten percentage points, or around six times the magnitude.

What has happened to the underlying distribution of incomes?

The fact that tax and benefit reforms have contained what would otherwise have been a considerably bigger increase in inequality of net incomes is consistent with the hypothesis that the underlying distribution of incomes has become more unequal over recent years. However, further analysis suggests the distribution of household pre-tax, non-benefit income has not become more unequal since 1996–7. Figure 5.7 shows the pattern of change in the Gini coefficient for gross income, i.e. household equivalised income measured before tax, and not including benefits.[11] For comparison, Figure 5.7 also shows the actual and simulated Gini coefficients for net income.

While incomes other than those from the state are much more unequally distributed than net incomes – the overall effect of direct taxes, tax credits and benefits is to redistribute from richer to poorer households – the main point to be taken from Figure 5.7 is that inequality in this measure of income has not risen over the period in question, but instead has remained flat.

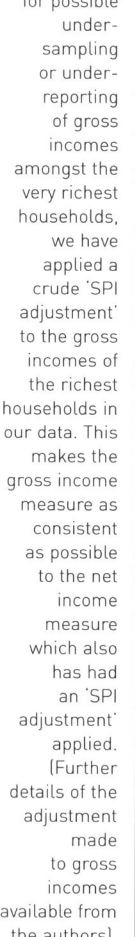

11 In order to correct for possible under-sampling or under-reporting of gross incomes amongst the very richest households, we have applied a crude 'SPI adjustment' to the gross incomes of the richest households in our data. This makes the gross income measure as consistent as possible to the net income measure which also has had an 'SPI adjustment' applied. (Further details of the adjustment made to gross incomes available from the authors).

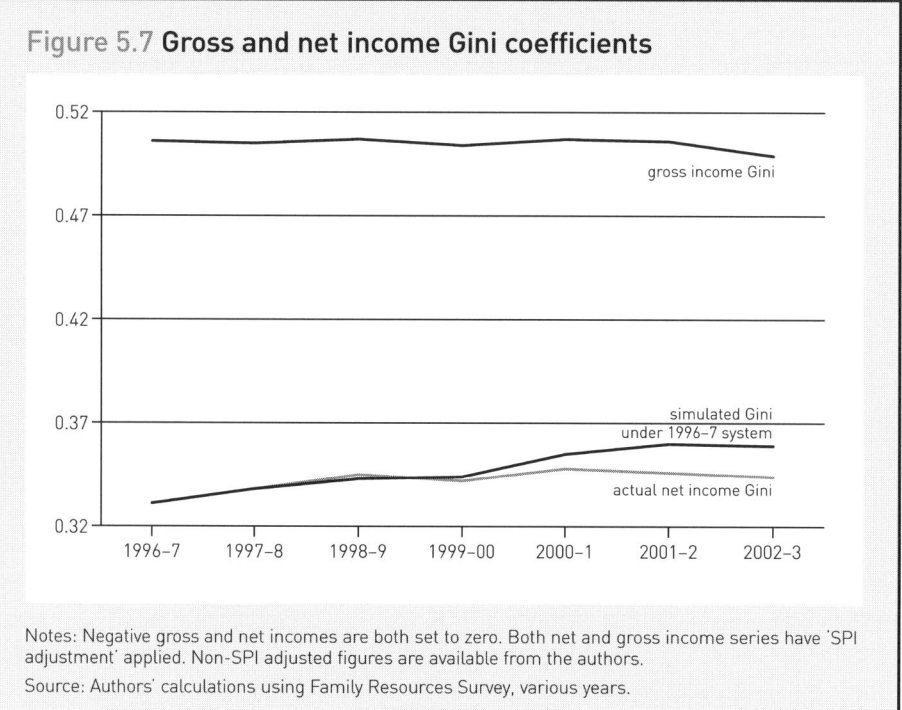

Figure 5.7 **Gross and net income Gini coefficients**

Notes: Negative gross and net incomes are both set to zero. Both net and gross income series have 'SPI adjustment' applied. Non-SPI adjusted figures are available from the authors.

Source: Authors' calculations using Family Resources Survey, various years.

That the gap between the gross and actual net income Gini coefficients (illustrated in Figure 5.7) has remained more or less constant over time, despite the increasing progressivity of the tax and benefit system is due to the stage in the economic cycle of our period of analysis, and in particular due to the falling unemployment over this time. During periods of falling unemployment, the amount of redistribution effected by a given tax and benefit system will tend to decline. However, progressive tax and benefit reforms have worked in the opposite direction, keeping the amount of redistribution done roughly constant.

Although overall inequality in household equivalised gross incomes has not gone up, the distributions of some specific sources of household income have continued to become more unequal in recent years. Figure 5.8 shows the Gini coefficient for each of the major income sources making up total gross income.

As Figure 5.8 shows, some sources of income are much more unequally distributed than others. For example, the distribution of household savings and investment income is very unequal compared to other sources of income. This is because most households who have savings and investment incomes receive only very small amounts of income from their savings, but there are also a significant number of households receiving very

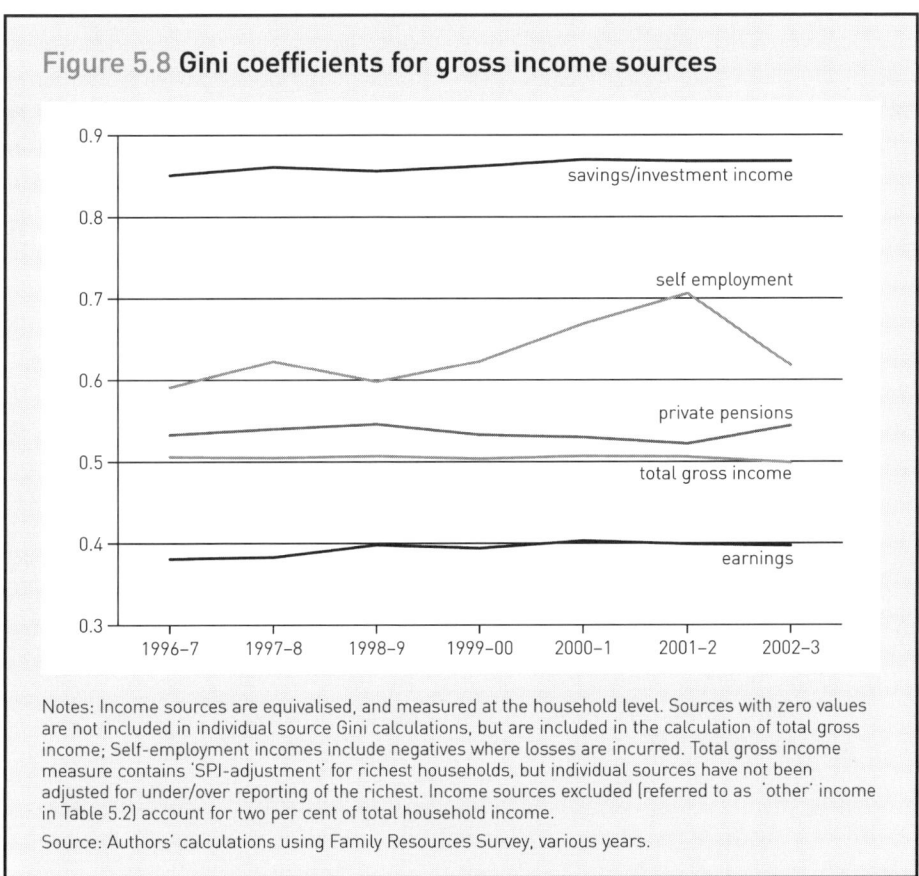

Figure 5.8 **Gini coefficients for gross income sources**

Notes: Income sources are equivalised, and measured at the household level. Sources with zero values are not included in individual source Gini calculations, but are included in the calculation of total gross income; Self-employment incomes include negatives where losses are incurred. Total gross income measure contains 'SPI-adjustment' for richest households, but individual sources have not been adjusted for under/over reporting of the richest. Income sources excluded (referred to as 'other' income in Table 5.2) account for two per cent of total household income.

Source: Authors' calculations using Family Resources Survey, various years.

Table 5.2 Share of total income, by income source, 2002–3

	Share of gross equivalised income	Share of net equivalised income
Earnings	76%	61%
Benefits	–	17%
Self-employment	11%	10%
Private pensions	7%	6%
Savings and investments	4%	4%
Other	2%	3%
Total	**100%**	**100%**

Notes: Income shares calculated on basis of non-SPI adjusted gross and net incomes. Net income shares calculated before the deduction of council tax. The share of total income made up by different sources has been relatively stable since 1996–7.

Source: Authors' calculations using Family Resources Survey, 2002–3.

large investment incomes. Self-employment incomes are also relatively unequally distributed. However these sources of income each make up a relatively small share of total gross income compared to earnings (Table 5.2). Household earnings are the most equally distributed income source.

Although a rise in inequality in one source of income does not necessarily imply an increase in overall inequality (since its contribution also depends on how this source of income is correlated with total income, and its share in total income), looking at how inequality in different income sources has changed is informative. In particular it highlights the fact that the distribution of equivalised household earnings, which makes up the biggest share of household income became slightly more unequal during the period of the Labour government. Reasons why such widening earnings inequality has continued over the 1990s and early 2000s are particularly associated with increases in the relative demand for more educated workers (see Machin (2003)), but have also been associated with other factors, such as changes to 'social norms' regarding top pay (see Piketty and Saez (2003), who put this forward as a possible explanation for recent changes in the income distribution in the US). Self-employment incomes have also become somewhat more unequal over this time.

Conclusions

Since the mid–1990s, Britain has experienced an unusual combination of slightly rising income inequality and falling relative poverty. This combination has arisen because of two trends: over the majority of the income distribution, growth in income has been slightly stronger amongst poorer individuals than for those located further up the income scale; but in the richest and poorest decile groups, the pattern is reversed, thereby increasing inequality. We have shown that this pattern of change is quite different from that of the 1980s, when incomes widened across the whole population and relative poverty rates grew rapidly.

The government has played an important role in making this unusual combination come about. Our analysis has shown that tax and benefit policy has kept the lid on what would otherwise have been a considerably bigger growth in after tax income inequality. Most notably, increases in means-tested benefits and tax credits directed towards low-income pensioners and families with children mean that some of the largest gains in income have been seen in the third decile of the distribution. Increases in employment rates have also contributed to this.

Although without Labour's tax and benefit reforms, the distribution of net incomes would have become more unequal than has occurred, inequality in income before taxes and benefits has remained relatively stable over this time. But inequality in some specific components of household income, most notably household earnings and self-employment has continued to rise slightly.

Redistribution through taxes and benefits, together with employment growth, has also put child poverty rates on a firm downward path. It looks as if the government is on course to meet its existing target to cut relative child poverty by one quarter by 2004–5. Pensioners have also seen their relative position continue to improve and, as a group, they are no longer any more likely to be poor than non-pensioners, measuring incomes after housing costs.

But not everyone has gained to the same extent. As we have shown, across the whole population, the incomes of the bottom fifteen per cent of the population have, on average, risen more slowly than those of the rest of the population. Perhaps as a result of this, our other work has shown that the poverty gap, which measures the depth of poverty amongst those who remain poor, has not become any smaller as poverty rates have declined. The declines in poverty are also limited to the government's favoured groups: relative poverty rates amongst those under pension age who are not parents – a group that includes almost two-fifths of the population – have not decreased, although they remain lower than poverty rates for children (see Brewer *et al.*, 2004).

How much will be achieved by the next set of government poverty targets? Achieving further big relative poverty reductions (which are required by the new poverty targets) through tax and benefit changes remains a formidable task. Government policy is also likely to try to make the underlying income distribution less unequal – for example, through investments in education and other policies aimed at improving the life chances of people from low-income backgrounds. More work is required to understand how large an impact this is likely to have both on the poverty measures targeted, and on income inequality, and the timescale required.

References

Atkinson, A. (2003) 'Top incomes in the United Kingdom over the twentieth century' University of Oxford, Nuffield College *mimeo* Available at www.nuff.ox.ac.uk/users/atkinson/TopIncomes20033.pdf

Brewer, M., Clark, T. and Wakefield, M. (2002) *Five years of social security reforms in the UK* Institute for Fiscal Studies, Working Paper W02/12. Available at www.ifs.org.uk/workingpapers/wp0212.pdf

Clark, T. and Taylor, J. (1999) 'Income Inequality: A tale of two cycles?' *Fiscal Studies* 20:387–408

Department for Work and Pensions (2004) *Households Below Average Income 1994–5 to 2002–3* Leeds: Corporate Document Services

Machin, S. (2003), 'Wage inequality since 1975' in R. Dickens, P. Gregg and J. Wadsworth (eds.) *The Labour Market under New Labour* Basingstoke and New York: Palgrave Macmillan

Piketty, T. and Saez, E. (2003) 'Income inequality in the United States 1913–1998' *Quarterly Journal of Economics* 118:1–39

6 Pay inequality and gender

Susan Harkness

In April 2004 the gender gap in pay stood at a recorded low of eighteen percentage points for full-time workers.[1] Since 1990 the pay gap has narrowed considerably, with the gap falling by six percentage points. This is a dramatic change since the early 1970s, when women working either full or part-time earned on average forty per cent less than men; and a substantial improvement since the early 1990s when the full-time pay gap stood at twenty-five per cent. For women working part-time however, progress has been much slower with the pay gap standing at a massive forty per cent for over a decade. This chapter documents changes in women's relative earnings over recent decades, paying particular attention to changes in gender (in)equality that have occurred since the Labour government came to power in 1997. It starts by looking at what has happened to the aggregate, full-time and part-time gender earnings ratios since the late 1970s. It then goes on to look at how the experiences of different groups of women have varied over time. Five key issues are focussed on and these look at women at different points of the wage distribution, with different levels of education, of different ages, from different generations and with and without children.[2]

While no policies have been introduced to directly tackle the problem of the gender pay gap since the late 1970s,[3] since 1997 a series of policy reforms have been introduced which are likely to have disproportionately affected women. Policy reforms have included the improvement of maternity, paternity and family leave provision, the introduction of the minimum wage, the extension of rights for part-time workers and the encouragement of large employers to undertake pay audits. At the same time there have been other longer-term changes that have affected women's relative labour market performance. Of particular importance is the change in educational attainment of girls and boys. Throughout the 1980s and 1990s the educational gap between girls and boys has been closing, with girls outperforming boys at school across the board by the end of the 1990s. Today more girls than boys enter university, while significantly fewer leave school without any qualifications.[4] A second important change is that women are increasingly having fewer children and giving birth at a later age. This, together with the fact that women are increasingly likely to work when they have young children, means that they now have fewer and shorter career interruptions. For more recent generations of women therefore differences in work experience should be a decreasingly important factor in explaining the pay gap.

The labour market contexts in which these changes have taken place are also important. First, since the late 1990s, high levels of employment

1 Source: Annual Survey of Hours and Earnings 2004 mean pay gap.

2 I would like to thank Alissa Goodman for helpful comments, the ESRC Data Archive for providing the data, and the Economic and Social Research Council (Research Grant R000223669].

3 In 1970 the Equal Pay Act was followed by the Sex Discrimination Act in 1975.

4 Source: Department for Education and Skills.

have been attained for the population as a whole, although employment growth has been particularly rapid for lone parents and mothers with children under five (Gregg and Harkness, 2003). Second, while it is well known that wage inequality grew rapidly throughout the 1980s, recent studies show that inequality continued to increase in the 1990s albeit at a slower rate. Studies suggest that those at the top of the wage distribution have 'broken away' from the rest with extremely rapid wage growth. However, while throughout the 1980s the lowest paid were continually falling behind those in the middle of the wage distribution, since the mid-1990s this erosion in the relative wages of low paid men has halted its decline. Finally, there has been a continued decline in manufacturing sector employment and a rise in employment in the service sector. Goos and Manning (2003) argue that changes in labour market demand have led to a growth in 'lovely and lousy' jobs. In particular they argue that jobs in the middle 'job quality' deciles have seen falls in their job shares, while there have been sharp increases in demand for those employed in the top and very bottom job quality deciles. As these bottom deciles are typically made up of 'female' service sectors jobs (including cleaners, hairdressing, sales assistants, beauticians, checkout assistants and waitresses) this expansion in demand is likely to have benefited some of the lowest paid women.

Changes in the aggregate, full-time and part-time pay gap

Since the 1990s the pay gap has closed substantially for those working full-time. This is shown in Figure 6.1, which plots the ratio of hourly earnings for all women employees, and for those working full and part-time, relative to the average full-time hourly male wage. Two data sets are used, the General Household Survey (GHS) and the Labour Force Survey (LFS). For full-time working women relative earnings have increased from just over sixty per cent in 1974 to eighty-two per cent in 2004. This change had two main phases: first pay increased substantially around the time of the 1975 Sex Discrimination Act, reaching seventy per cent by 1982, where after the ratio remained stable until 1991; since 1991 the ratio has seen a continual and sustained climb.[5] For women working part-time, however, relative pay has changed little over the last thirty years. In both 1974 and 1998 women working part-time earned just over sixty per cent of the average full-time hourly male wage.[6] Data from the LFS suggest a slightly higher earnings ratio for part time workers,[7] but does not indicate a significant improvement in relative earnings since 1992. While the hourly pay gap for full-time workers has narrowed, because men on average work longer hours than women, the gap in earnings is larger and the improvement in pay smaller when weekly or annual measures of earnings are used. In 2004 the earnings ratio falls

5 For full-time employees, the LFS data suggests a pay gap of eighteen percentage points in 2004. This is the same as the gap reported from the Annual Survey of Hours and Earnings data set, the largest and most precise source of earnings data, which is available from 1998.

6 The Annual Survey of Hours and Earnings provides the most precise estimates of the part-time pay gap, but is available only from 1998. It estimates the part-time earnings ratio to be sixty per cent in April 2004. In 2004 part-time women earned on average ten per cent less than part-time men.

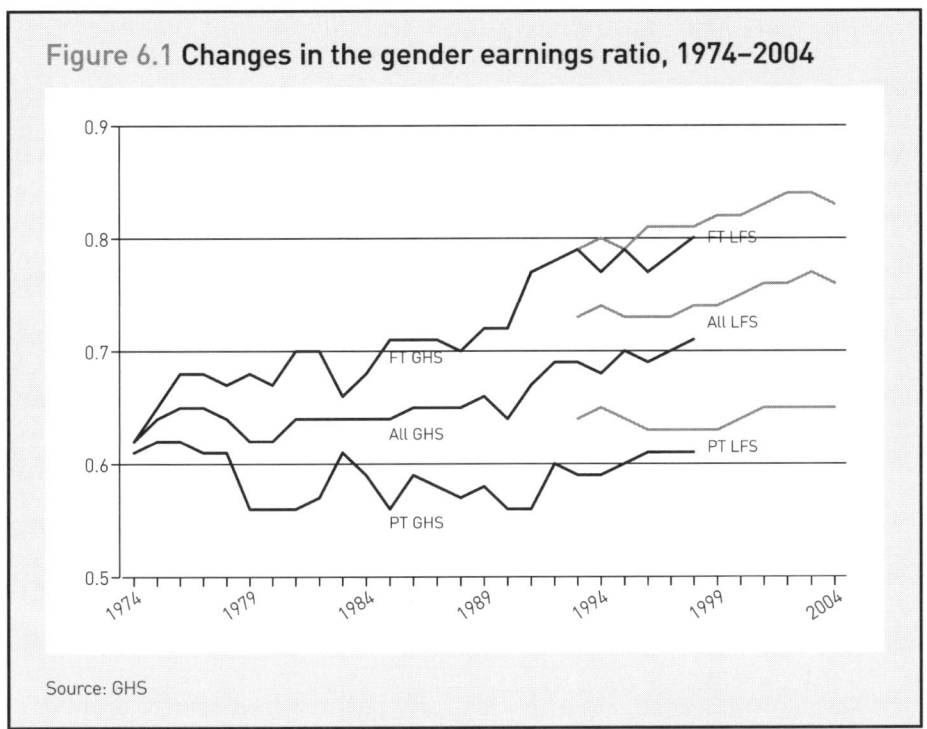

Figure 6.1 **Changes in the gender earnings ratio, 1974–2004**

Source: GHS

from 82.1 for hourly earnings to 75.5 per cent for weekly earnings and 72.1 per cent for annual earnings.

Recent studies show that little of the difference in pay between men and women working full-time can be explained by differences in measurable characteristics (see Harkness 1996).[8] In particular Harkness finds that differences in human capital only account for a substantial part of the full-time pay gap for older women working in the 1970s. By the 1990s, human capital differences did little to explain the gap at any age. At any point in time therefore the majority of the full-time pay gap is attributable to differences in 'unobserved' characteristics (such as 'effort') and 'discrimination'. These findings also suggest that the recent decline in the full-time pay gap must primarily have resulted either from a reduction in 'discrimination' or a convergence in unobserved characteristics of male and female full-time employees (for example, as a result of increased labour market attachment of women). For part-time workers however there is little evidence of direct discrimination. Indeed differences in observed characteristics explain almost all the gap in pay between those working full and part-time (Harkness 1996; Manning and Petrongolo 2004). According to Manning and Petrongolo a typical part-time employee has a low level of education, has a partner and young and numerous dependent children and works in a low-level occupation.

7 Manning and Petrongolo (2004) discuss in detail differences in the estimated part-time penalty when different data sources are used.

8 These measured characteristics typically include a quadratic in age, a set of education dummy variables, a quadratic in work experience, years of work experience, and dummy variables for industry and occupation.

The wage distribution

While full-time working women's average earnings caught up with those of men by a substantial amount in the 1990s and early noughties, changes at the mean may disguise differences among subgroups of workers or variations in progress at different parts of the wage distribution. An analysis of the full earnings distribution for men and women shows just how much earnings have converged over the last decade. What is remarkable is the extent to which by 2001–2 the earnings distribution of full-time working women has collapsed onto that for men. For part-time workers, inequality has risen (as it also has for men and women working fulltime). However the women distribution remains mainly at substantially lower wages than that for men.

An analysis of the relative earnings of men and women across the wage distribution allows us to compare the richest and poorest men and women. It shows that the lowest paid full-time working women have higher relative earnings than women higher up the wage distribution, and that they have seen the most substantial improvement in their relative pay. These low paid women (in the bottom decile of the earnings distribution) are predominantly young (one-third are under twenty-two), two-thirds work part-time, half have O levels or GCSEs or under, forty per cent have two or more children and the vast majority (over ninety per cent) work in the service sector. The improvement in their relative earnings may reflect the fact that those in low paid service sector and non-routine occupations have seen an increase in demand for their labour (Goos and Manning), while the minimum wage may also have boosted their relative pay as disproportionately more low-paid women than men benefited from its introduction.

At the other end of the wage distribution, women are doing less well. While relative pay has improved continually for women at all points of the wage distribution, for women at the top the improvement is less marked and the gender pay ratio starts to decline beyond the 80th percentile. This is a relatively recent change and may reflect the fact that women have not been party to the 'take off' in earnings observed for men at the very top of the wage distribution.

Education

Differences observed across the wage distribution suggest that there may also be important differences in earnings between men and women with different levels of education. In the past it has historically been the case that the pay gap has been smaller for more educated women. This could be explained by the fact that those women who had decided to stay on in education were likely to exhibit a high degree of labour market attachment. Figure 6.2 shows how the pay gap has changed over time for all women and for those working full-time with (i) less than five O levels or GCSEs, (ii)

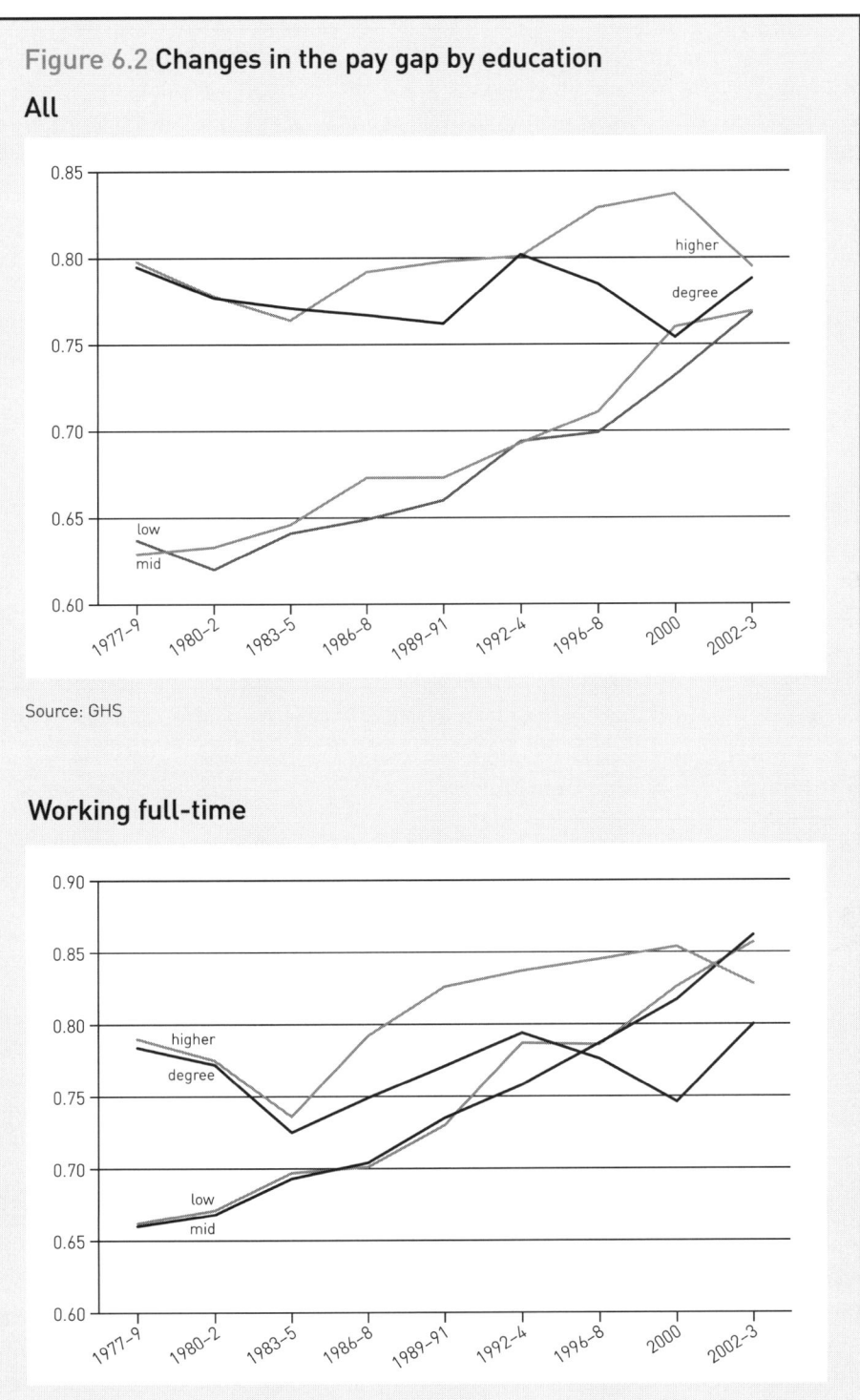

Figure 6.2 **Changes in the pay gap by education**

All

Source: GHS

Working full-time

Source: GHS

more than five O-levels or GCSEs but fewer than two A levels, (iii) two or more A levels but less than a degree, and (iv) a degree or higher. For women with degrees or higher education the pay gap is high, at between seventy-five and eighty per cent, throughout the twenty-five years period for which we have data. However there is little improvement in the relative earnings of these women. On the other hand for those with lower levels of qualifications the pay gap has steadily decreased from around sixty-three per cent to seventy-seven per cent. Looking only at those working full-time, a similar pattern is observed although and the pay ratios are slightly higher. Over the last two decades, and in particular over the 1990s and early noughties, the biggest gains in relative earning have been for the less well educated. One explanation for this may be that while highly educated women have always had high rates of employment, if employment rates are also rising among less educated women then their relative wages may rise. Employment data does not however support this explanation. Full-time employment rates of the less educated remain far behind those of women with higher education. Moreover there is no catch-up over the decades. Less skilled women are much more likely to work part time, although there has been some rise in part time work among better qualified women (although not among those with degrees). That there has been no gain in employment suggests that the main explanation of the observed rise in relative earnings for less educated workers reflects the growth in demand for low-skilled non-routine service sector labour, and policy changes such as the minimum wage which have disproportionately benefited these women.

Wages, age and year of birth

Wages and age

Historically the gender pay gap has widened with age. One plausible explanation for this may be that women's earnings fall behind those of men with age because the difference in years of work experience gained widens as a result of career interruptions. An alternative explanation might be that women fall increasingly behind over time because they have are less likely to be promoted, so that while male wages tend to increase with age for women this rate of increase is likely to be much slower. In 1979–80, wages were similar for all at the time of labour market entry (around age twenty), but for those just five years older a substantial pay gap had emerged. Indeed while male earnings grew with age up to their mid to late-thirties, for women earnings had peaked by the age of thirty for those working full-time and by twenty-five for those working part-time. This pattern has however changed over time as male and female earnings have converged. By 2001–2 the earnings of full-time working women aged under thirty were similar to those of young men and only after the age of thirty does a notable difference in wages emerge (with male earnings growing with age up until forty-five, while for women working full-time earnings peaked by around thirty-five). For women work-ing part-time some increase in earnings occurs with age, although at all ages earnings are far behind those of full-time employees.

While the pay gap for women working full-time tends to increase with age, the rate at which it increases had slowed substantially by 2001–2. Between 1979–80 and 2001–2 there was a substantial rise in the relative earnings of women at all ages, but the biggest gains were concentrated on women in their thirties. Thus while in the 1970s women in their twenties working full-time earned around seventy-five per cent of the male wage, this proportion fell to sixty-five per cent for those in their thirties and for-ties. By 2001–2 full-time women in their twenties earned as much as men, while those in their thirties earned ninety per cent of the male wage and those over forty earned around eighty per cent of the male wage. For part-time workers, earnings are low relative to male wages at all ages, other than for the very young, because part-time earnings do not tend to rise with age.

There are several plausible explanations for the catch up of female to male earnings. First women's earnings may have caught up with those of men because women are now more attached to the labour market. Changes in patterns of fertility and employment mean that women now have fewer and shorter career breaks, and this may mean that as women age they fall behind men in the labour market more slowly. Full-time employment rates rise substantially for those aged between twenty-five and fifty-five, with the largest gains in employment for women in their thirties. This supports the hypothesis that increased work experience may have helped reduce the pay gap.

A second explanation for the observed change in the age related pay gap may be that differences in skills between men and women have been narrowing. In particular girls have caught up boys in terms of their edu-cational attainment. The latest figures for England in 2003–4 show that forty-nine per cent of boys achieved five or more GCSEs at grades A* to C compared to fifty-nine per cent of girls. Andrews et al. (2004) argue that girls overtook boys after the introduction of the GCSE examination system in 1988, and that this change alongside other educational reforms may have favoured girls. Among those entered for A levels, girls do better too: in 2003–4 ninety-three per cent of girls entered for A levels achieved two or more passes compared to ninety-one per cent of boys. While this gap is small compared to that for achievement at age sixteen, girls have done better than boys throughout the 1990s. This improvement in the relative education of girls would be expected to lead to a narrowing of the pay gap among the young over recent decades. A third explanation for the observed catch-up in pay may be that successive birth cohorts are entering the labour market with different attitudes towards work and families, with greater labour market attachment and greater equality at home. Thus while earlier generations of women fell behind men because of longer and more frequent career interruptions associated with child birth, more recent generations may be closing the gap with men because they have more similar employment profiles. This may be expected to lead to improved relative pay over time, and these changes may be expected to persist across generations. These generation effects are explored in greater detail below.

Changes across generations

In this section we look at how earnings of women have evolved with age relative to men for those born in five different birth cohorts (1935–9, 1945–9, 1955–9, 1965–9 and 1975–9). As we only have data for 1974–2002, we are unable to observe full wage-age profiles for each of our cohorts. Instead we observe wages from ages thirty-six to fifty-nine for the 1935–39 cohort and from age sixteen to twenty-seven for the 1975–9 cohort. For the intervening cohorts we observe more complete data and are therefore able to make some comparisons across cohorts. For the oldest birth cohort (1935–9) we first observe wages at the age of thirty-five. For this cohort by the age of thirty-five a substantial gap in earnings had emerged. Wages continue to grow with age (and time) and substantial gender differences in earnings remain. For the 1945–9 and 1955–9 birth cohorts we are able to observe a slightly longer series of wage data. For the 1945–9 cohort large wage differences are observed at all ages for which we have data (i.e. from age twenty-five to fifty-nine onwards). From the 1955–9 cohort on we begin to observe wages on entry to the labour market and interesting wage patterns emerge. In particular we see that for the 1955–9 cohort labour market entry wages (at around ages sixteen to twenty) are similar for men and women. However a pay gap emerges by the time these women reach their early twenties, and carries on widening beyond the age of thirty for those working full-time. For those working part-time wages fall behind at an earlier age, as earnings grow much less rapidly with age or time. Those born in 1965–9 do better than earlier cohorts, while for the latest cohort, 1975–9, wages are indistinguishable for men and women working full-time for the entire period over which they are observed.

Translating this wage data into earnings ratios reveals some very clear patterns emerging across cohorts. For each cohort there has been a substantial gain in relative earnings among those working full-time. For those cohorts that we are able to observe on entry into the labour market we find that each successive generation has entered the labour market less disadvantaged than before. Moreover while there is some small dip in earnings at the start of women's careers, beyond this there is little further evidence of declining relative wages with age among those working full-time. Thus the 'experience' hypothesis, which suggests that the pay gap widens with age as a result of a widening of the experience gap, does not seem to be well supported by the data. Instead, and in line with findings in the US by

Weinberger and Kuhn (2004), the patterns observed suggest that successive cohorts are entering the labour market with higher relative wages, and that this gain is being maintained as these women age. Of particular note is the improvement in relative earnings of the 1955–9 cohort. This cohort sees a large jump in relative earnings, and a plausible explanation for this leap is that this generation was the first to enter the labour market after the implementation of the Equal Pay and Sex Discrimination Acts. These women therefore entered the labour market with a substantial improvement in relative earnings (compared to earlier generations), and this gain in earnings appears to have been maintained as the cohort aged. For those already in the labour market however there was little jump in earnings associated with the introduction of this legislation.

These cross cohort changes are central to explaining the recent decline in the pay gap, and suggest that it is not the case that new generations of women are entering the labour market with similar earnings to men and then falling behind. Instead improvements in relative pay appear to be being driven primarily by a decline in the pay gap across cohorts. The implication of these finding are that the gender earnings gap will continue to decline as older cohorts of women age out of the labour market.

Mothers

A final area of policy concern is the 'family gap' in pay. This describes earnings differences between women with and without children. It is well known that in the UK there is a pay penalty to motherhood (see Joshi *et al.*, 1999) and that this penalty is larger in the UK than in many other OECD countries (Harkness and Waldfogel 2003). Policy reforms over recent years which have improved support for childcare and working parents, and extended maternity leave provision, may have had an impact on this earnings gap. Figure 6.3 plots the earnings of mothers and women without children relative to men for those aged between twenty-five and forty-four. The raw data suggests that the pay penalty to having children is closing both for those working full and part-time, and that this narrowing has occurred mainly from 1998 on.

In order to take account of differences in employment characteristics, and to estimate the 'penalty' to having children a regression of the log wage is run on a set of 'human capital' characteristics.[9] The results are reported in Table 6.1. In 1989–90 the estimated pay penalty to having children stood at seven per cent for those working full-time with one child, twelve per cent for two children and twenty-four per cent for three. By 2001–2 this gap had declined to such an extent that for those working full-time there was no pay penalty associated with having just one child, although for those with two or more children a significant penalty remained (of ten per cent for two children and fifteen per cent for those with three or more). Policy reforms

9 Controls include a quadratic in age, eleven regional dummy variables, education dummy variables and controls for industry. Data is from the GHS.

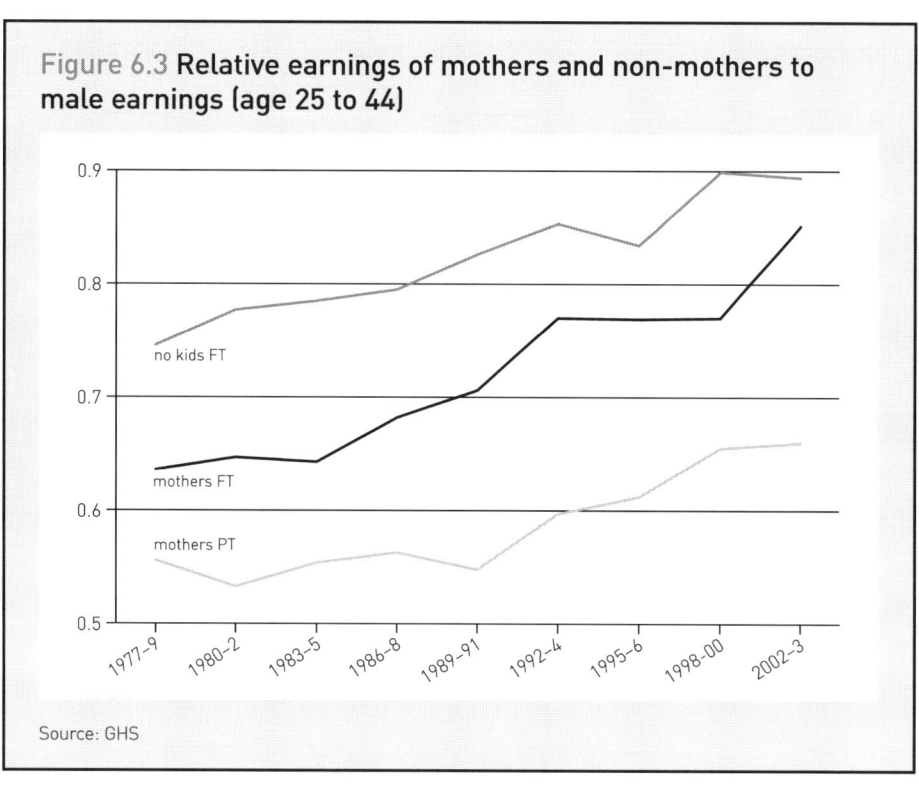

Figure 6.3 **Relative earnings of mothers and non-mothers to male earnings (age 25 to 44)**

no kids FT

mothers FT

mothers PT

Source: GHS

Table 6.1 **The pay penalty to having children**

	1989–90		2001–2	
	All	FT	All	FT
One child	10.0%	6.6%	4.0%	None
Two children	20.0%	12.3%	13.6%	10.0%
Three or more children	24.5%	24.2%	19.5%	15.0%

therefore do appear to have benefited mothers, although these benefits are less pronounced for those with larger families and for women who work part-time.

Conclusions

While the pay gap has narrowed over recent decades, this chapter highlights how the pay gap varies both across the wage distribution and across different groups of workers, and how these differences have changed with time. In the early 1990s we have seen that the pay gap was smallest for better educated workers, the young, those without children and those who worked full-time. Since the early 1990s the largest gains in relative earnings have been seen among low-paid and less well-educated, women in their thirties and early forties, and mothers who work full-time. Those who have seen the smallest gains are those working part-time, older women, women at the top of the pay distribution who have hit the 'glass ceiling', and mothers who have more than one child. These findings suggest that future policy should focus on these groups, while at the same time ensuring that young cohorts are able to maintain their early gains.

References

Andrews, M., Bradley, S., Stott, D. and Taylor J. (2004) 'The Evolution and Determination of the Gender Gap in Education' Nuffield Foundation Education Seminar

Goos, M. and Manning A. (2003) 'Lousy and Lovely Jobs: The rising polarisation of work in Britain' *CEP Discussion Paper 604*, London School of Economics, December 2003

Gregg, P. and Harkness, S. (2003) 'Welfare Reform and Lone Parents Employment in the UK' *Working Paper 03/072*, Centre for Market and Public Organisation, University of Bristol

Harkness, S. (1996) 'The Gender Earnings Gap: Evidence from the UK' *Fiscal Studies* 17(2) May 1996

Harkness, S. and Waldfogel, J. (2003) 'The Family Gap in Pay: Evidence from seven industrialised countries' *Research in Labor Economics* 22:369-414

Joshi, H., Paci, P. and Waldfogel, J. (1999) 'The Wages of Motherhood: Better or worse?' *Cambridge Journal of Economics* 23(5):543-564

7 Maintaining momentum in tackling child poverty

Mike Brewer

The government should meet its target to reduce child poverty by a quarter from its level in 1998–9 by 2004–5, although we will not know for certain until Spring 2006. But, under the government's current assumptions about future spending on tax credits, relative child poverty will then rise. An increase in spending on tax credits and means-tested benefits of around two billion pounds a year by 2007–8 would put the government back on track to meet its target for child poverty in 2010. Achieving the same reduction without further damaging parents' financial incentives to work, however, would cost more.

There is a risk, though, that focusing on a measure of child poverty defined in terms of family incomes downgrades the role that public services can play in improving the life chances of deprived children. Arguably, the government should now be considering what would most help reduce child poverty in 2020. Given that the majority of those who will be parents in 2020 are currently at school, measures that improve social mobility may well have a greater long-term pay-back in the fight against child poverty.[1]

Government target for 2004–5 to be met

The government has a target for child poverty to fall by a quarter of its level in 1998–9 by 2004–5, which it should meet. For the purposes of the target, a child is counted as poor if it lives in a household with less than sixty per cent median income, where incomes are measured both before and after housing costs have been deducted (respectively referred to as BHC and AHC). Incomes are adjusted using the McClements equivalence scale.

Measuring incomes AHC, 4.2 million children lived in households with less than sixty per cent median income in 1998–9; measuring incomes BHC, the figure is 3.1 million children. These imply targets for 2004–5 of 3.1 million and 2.3 million respectively.

Most commentators agree with the government's assessment in the 2003 Pre-Budget Report that the government should meet its child poverty target for 2004–5, not least because the government has increased transfers to low-income families with children since 1997 by almost one per cent of GDP, an historically unprecedented amount.[1] However, there are uncertainties in making these forecasts, not least because the government uses a survey of around 30,000 households to estimate child poverty in a population roughly 1,000 times as large. Analysis shows that the target should be met comfortably measuring incomes BHC, but there is less room for manoeuvre

1 I am very grateful to Will Paxton for suggesting the subject matter of the talk, and for attendees at the forum for comments. Support from the ESRC Centre for Microeconomic Analysis of Public Policy (CPP) at the IFS is gratefully acknowledged. The Households Below Average Income and the Family Resources Survey data sets are used with permission of the Department for Work and Pensions, which bears no responsibility for the views expressed here.

measuring incomes AHC. We should know for sure whether the target has been hit in spring 2006, when data on household incomes in 2004–5 is released.

Relative child poverty to rise

However, relative child poverty will then probably start to rise, given current policy assumptions. The government's next target is for child poverty in 2010–1 to be half its level in 1998–9. The definition of poverty will be different from that used for the target in 2004–5. In fact, three measures of poverty will be tracked:

- An absolute measure of child poverty, where a child is poor if it lives in a household with less than sixty per cent of the median income in 1998–9

- A relative measure of child poverty, where a child is poor if it lives in a household with less than sixty per cent of the contemporaneous median income

- A material deprivation measure of child poverty, where a child is poor if it lives in a household both with less than seventy per cent of the contemporaneous median income and experiences material deprivation.

The rest of this note focuses on the second of these, because reducing absolute child poverty is not considered to be particularly challenging, and because data does not yet exist to measure child poverty using the third definition (the government has promised to set a target for the material deprivation definition of child poverty during the 2006 Spending Review).

Another change made by the government for the 2010–1 target is that it will only measure income BHC (rather than both AHC and BHC), and it will use the Modified OECD Equivalence Scale. The latter change acts to increase levels of child poverty compared with the previously-used McClements' scale, but the former change means that the headline level of child poverty is lower than if the government focused on incomes measured AHC (Brewer *et al.*, 2004). The level of child poverty in 1998–9 using this measure was 3.4 million, so child poverty needs to be 1.7 million in 2010–1 to meet the target, a level not seen in the UK since the previous Labour government was in power, in 1978.

What will now happen to levels of child poverty? Assessing future levels of child poverty requires us to take a view on the likely distribution of income, and forecasting what might happen to the distribution of income by 2010–1 is extremely difficult. Household incomes are affected by numerous factors, including growth in earnings and unearned income, as well as changes in the population, household composition, patterns of employment, tax and benefit policies, and take-up of means-tested benefits and tax

2 See Cm 6042 (2003–4 session) and Adam and Brewer (2004) for details of the rise in child-contingent support. The government's assessment of child poverty in 2004–5 is in para 5.20 of Cm 6042 (2003–4 session). The IFS assessment was given in evidence to the Work and Pensions Committee's enquiry into child poverty in the UK: see paras 133–136 of HC 85(i) (2003–4), or Brewer (2004a). An assessment was also made in Sutherland et al (2003).

3 The measures were announced in DWP (2003) and are analysed in chapter 4 of Brewer et al (2004).

credits. Some of these changes – such as increased employment amongst mothers – may well act to reduce child poverty, but others may increase median income, and this will also affect child poverty by raising the poverty line.

In this note, we ask an easier question: what might child poverty be in 2007–8, half-way between the current position and the date when the next target applies. To answer this, we forecast child poverty assuming that the population, employment rates and household composition do not change from their 2002–3 values (the latest year for which we have detailed information; data for 2003–4 will be available in spring 2005), but that real earnings do change over time in line with past trends.

This means that any forecast changes in child poverty can only be due to two factors:

■ changes in the level (but not the distribution) of earned income;

■ real changes in taxes and benefits that have already been announced by the government.

Previous work has shown that uniform growth in earnings (in other words, an equal percentage rise in earnings experienced by all workers and self-employed individuals) worsens relative child poverty, because earnings are a less important source of income for poor households with children than they are for the median household. See, for example, Brewer (2003) or Sutherland *et al.* (2003). In addition, the government's current assumptions for future rates of tax credits imply real cuts in the entitlements of low-income families with children from April 2006 onwards;[3] if confirmed in subsequent Budgets, these changes would increase child poverty further. The combined effect is that the number of children in poverty could be over 500,000 higher by 2007–8 than the government might wish if it wanted to keep child poverty on track for its 2010–1 target (see Figure 7.1).

Tackling child poverty vs parental work incentives

It could cost around two billion pounds a year to put child poverty back on track by 2007–8, but at the cost of worsening financial work incentives for parents.

There are many ways in which the government might alter taxes and benefits in 2007–8 to reduce child poverty. Previous work, though, has shown that increasing the per child element of the child tax credit is one of the most efficient policies, where efficiency is defined as the number of children lifted out of poverty per pound spent (see, for example, Brewer (2004b). Our estimates suggest that an increase in the per child element of the Child Tax Credit of £300 a year would be sufficient to put child poverty back on track by 2007–8, at a cost of around two billion pounds

4 Estimates of future spending on tax credits made in the 2004 Pre-Budget Report assume that the per child element of the child tax credit and most elements of the working tax credit rise in line with inflation, but that the family element of the child tax credit and the income thresholds are frozen, implying small real cuts in entitlements overall. The overall impact would be to reduce tax credit awards for all families with children by around £250 million a year, for each year that this policy is in effect, compared to a policy of indexing all thresholds and credits in line with inflation: see Brewer (2004a).

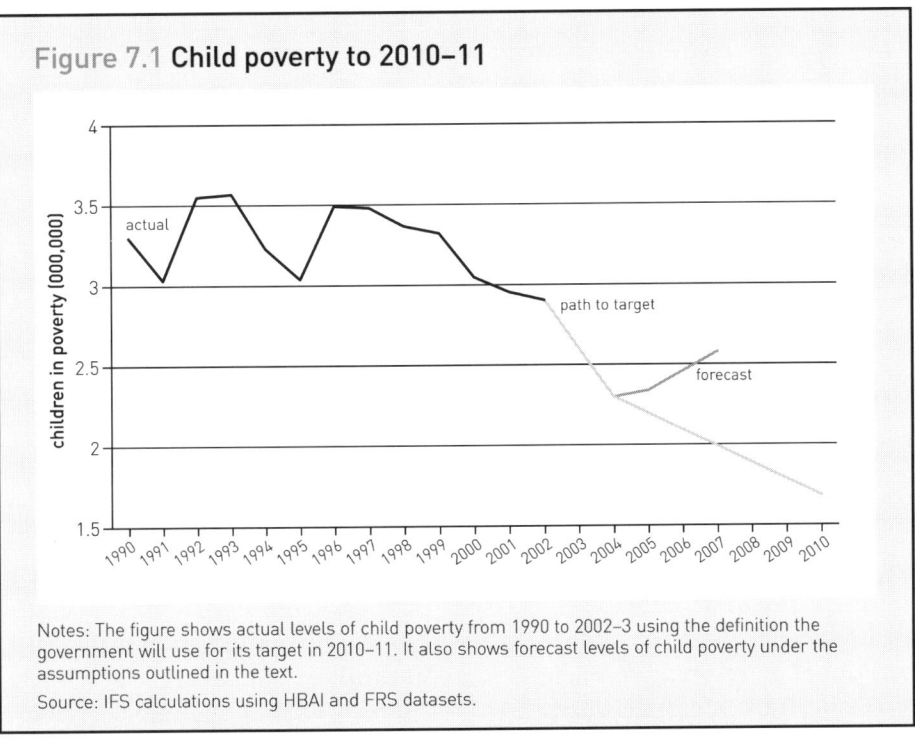

Figure 7.1 **Child poverty to 2010–11**

children in poverty (000,000)

actual

path to target

forecast

1990 1991 1992 1993 1994 1995 1996 1997 1998 1999 2000 2001 2002 2003 2004 2005 2006 2007 2008 2009 2010

Notes: The figure shows actual levels of child poverty from 1990 to 2002–3 using the definition the government will use for its target in 2010–11. It also shows forecast levels of child poverty under the assumptions outlined in the text.

Source: IFS calculations using HBAI and FRS datasets.

a year (both values in current prices, and assuming that child allowances in means-tested benefits rise commensurately). This is not a substantial increase when compared with the changes in child-contingent support since 1997, but it is a substantial sum given the current state of the public finances: although the government is forecasting that it will meet its fiscal rules during the next economic cycle, this relies on a strong rise in tax revenues which some commentators doubt will materialise (see Chote and Emmerson (2004)).

However, increases in the per child element of the Child Tax Credit worsen, on average, the financial work incentives facing parents in low-income families. This is both because such a change would reduce the financial gain to working at all for some parents, and because such a rise would increase the proportion of parents for whom a rise in earnings is offset by a reduction in tax credit award; these effects are more likely to be experienced by parents in low to middle-income families than those in the top half of the income distribution.

Although the negative impact on financial work incentives may not be large, it is notable that the government's success in its first term in reforming taxes and benefits to make work pay for low-income families has been partially undermined by the focus in its second term in office on reducing child poverty by increasing the incomes available to families who do not work (see Brewer and Shephard (2004)). If the government does decide to increase the per child element of the child tax credit, it may find that the direct impact on child poverty may be partially undone by reductions in the labour supply of parents. Avoiding these negative implications for financial work incentives would be possible – for example, by increasing the working tax credit, or by increasing child benefit rather than income-related tax credits – but reducing child poverty and improving work incentives together can only be done at a price.[4]

Relative child poverty – a distraction?

Is the high profile target for relative child poverty drawing attention away from the government's targets for children's outcomes, and downgrading the role for public services in reducing child poverty?

The government's review of child poverty, published with the 2004 Spending Review, announced many targets relating to child poverty (see HM Treasury (2004), Appendix C). Many of these directly relate to children's outcomes, and are concerned with inequalities in these outcomes. For example, there are targets to reduce levels of and inequalities in infant mortality and life expectancy at birth, children's communication, social and emotional development by age five, education attainment at age eleven. Arguably, these are better measures of children's well-being than a measure of their parents' income.

Although these targets share the same status as the target for relative child poverty in 2010–1 – they are all Public Service Agreements, against which government departments supposedly need to show progress in when they agree future spending levels with the Treasury – there is no doubt that the measure of income poverty is the most high profile both amongst politicians and those concerned about child poverty outside government; this means that the temptation will always be to direct any extra resources that the government wants to devote to tackling child poverty towards increases in tax credits rather than into public services that improve the life-chances of deprived children. Although recent evidence suggests that parents are spending their extra state transfers on their children, we do not really know whether this extra money is translating into improved outcomes for these children, nor whether any such improvements could be obtained at lower cost through improvements in public services (see Gregg et al., (2005)).

Furthermore, given that the government is some six years away from its next target on relative child poverty, the government should arguably now be considering what policies would most help abolish child poverty by 2020. Given that the majority of those who will be parents in 2020 are probably currently at school or in higher education, measures that improve the social mobility of children may well have a greater pay-back in the long-term fight against child poverty.

5 This issue is being addressed directly in research funded by the JRF ongoing at the time of writing: see http://www.jrf.org.uk/knowledge/wip/record.asp?ID=802995.

References

Adam, S. and Brewer, M. (2004), *Supporting Families: The financial costs and benefits of children since 1975* Bristol: The Policy Press

Brewer, M. (2003) 'What do the child poverty targets mean for the child tax credit? An update' IFS Briefing Note 41. Available at http://www.ifs.org.uk/bns/bn41.pdf

Brewer, M. (2004a) 'Will the government hit its child poverty target in 2004/05?' IFS Briefing Note 47. Available at http://www.ifs.org.uk/bns/bn47.pdf

Brewer, M. (2004b) 'Child Poverty and Tax Credit Changes: A note for the Work and Pensions Select Committee' Available at http://www.publications.parliament.uk/pa/cm200304/cmselect/cmworpen/85/85-III/85we05.htm

Brewer, M., Goodman, A., Myck, M., Shaw, J. and Shephard, A. (2004) *Poverty and inequality in Britain: 2004* London: IFS

Chote, R. and Emmerson, C. (2004) 'Pre-Budget Report 2004' IFS Press Release. Available at http://www.ifs.org.uk/pr/pbr_pubfin.pdf

Cm 6042 (2003-04 session) *The Strength to Take the Long-term Decisions for Britain: Seizing the opportunities of the global recovery* London: The Stationery Office

Department for Work and Pensions (2003) *Measuring Child Poverty* London: DWP

Gregg, P., Waldfogel, J. and Washbrook, E. (2005) 'That's the Way the Money Goes: Expenditure patterns as real income rise for the poorest families with children' in J. Hills and K. Stewart (eds.) *An Equal Society? New Labour, poverty, inequality and exclusion* Bristol: The Policy Press

HC 85(i) (2003-04 session) *Child Poverty in the UK* London: The Stationery Office

HM Treasury (2004) *Child Poverty Review* London: The Stationery Office

Sutherland, H., Piachaud, D. and Sefton, T., (2003) *Poverty in Britain* York: YPS

8 The challenge of full employment
Peter Robinson

Employment opportunity for all is a precondition of a fair society. Social justice and full employment go hand in hand.
(Department for Work and Pensions, 2004)

The central role of full employment in achieving social justice was recognised long before ippr's Commission on Social Justice emphasised in 1994 that 'paid work for a fair wage is the most secure and sustainable way out of poverty' (CSR:20). Unsurprisingly, given the background of the 1930s, the 'post-war consensus' placed the maintenance of full employment at the centre of economic and social policy. It was the failure of governments after the mid-1970s to keep unemployment down that led many to the pessimistic conclusion that full employment was dead as an aspiration. It is the steady downward trend in unemployment since the early 1990s that has allowed policy makers to talk meaningfully again about getting back to full employment.

Indeed, the labour market has changed in two significant ways since that ippr Commission reported in 1994. Firstly, employment has risen and unemployment has fallen steadily since the end of the recession in 1993. Secondly, a less well noticed change that occurred at around the time of the Commission's report, is the ending of the sharp rise in wage inequality that took place from the late 1970s to the early 1990s. Labour market outcomes look much less threatening than they were in 1994. However, significant problems remain: economic inactivity is still high and although wage inequality is no longer rising so sharply, it is not falling either.

Why do we care about full employment? Clearly, worklessness is highly correlated with income poverty in the UK. Two-thirds of working age adults living in workless households had incomes below sixty per cent of the median (after housing costs) in 2002–3 compared with just seven per cent of adults in households where all the adults were in work (DWP/ONS, 2004). Of course this is in part due to the low levels of income replacement offered by the British benefits system; more generous out-of-work benefits could lift a higher proportion of workless households out of poverty.

However, we care about involuntary unemployment for reasons other than just the effect on income. Involuntary unemployment and the fear of unemployment has one of the biggest adverse impacts on self-reported measures of wellbeing and objective indicators of physical and mental health, as emphasised most recently by the research on 'happiness' (Burchardt, 2004; Di Tella *et al.*, 2002). This adverse effect becomes more severe the longer a person is out of work and the various scarring effects of unemployment can impact significantly on an individual's life chances. Although we need to know more about the impact of long periods of economic inactivity on wellbeing, as opposed to unemployment, anyone familiar with a century's worth of literature would not doubt the impact of worklessness. It is useful that more rigorous analysis has demonstrated that Orwell and Steinbeck retain some relevance and that unemployment continues to impact significantly on wellbeing today, despite dramatic improvements in overall living standards since the 1930s.

New Labour – a new definition of full employment?

Since 1997 the government's approach to the labour market has emphasised four explicit policy objectives and one implicit political objective.

Reducing unemployment and economic inactivity

Labour inherited an economy in 1997 where employment and unemployment rates had already been moving in the right direction since the end of the early 1990s recession (see Figures 8.1 and 8.2). The New Deal, as one of the government's early flagship initiatives, emphasised the importance of reducing youth unemployment, but was soon joined by a range of other New Deals aimed at different target groups. Policy increasingly

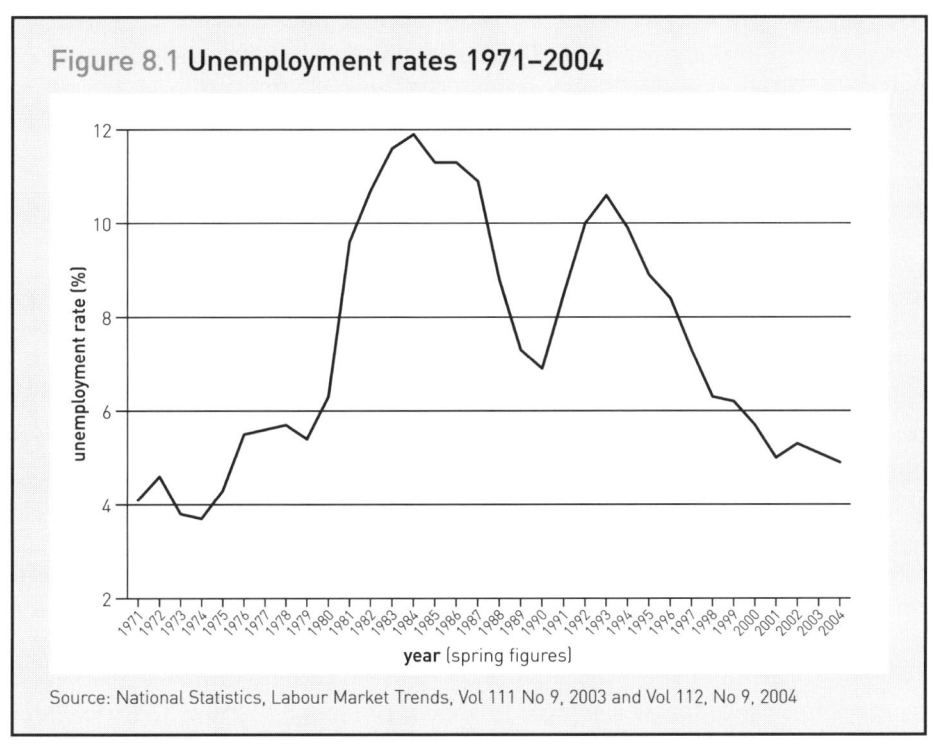

Figure 8.1 **Unemployment rates 1971–2004**

Source: National Statistics, Labour Market Trends, Vol 111 No 9, 2003 and Vol 112, No 9, 2004

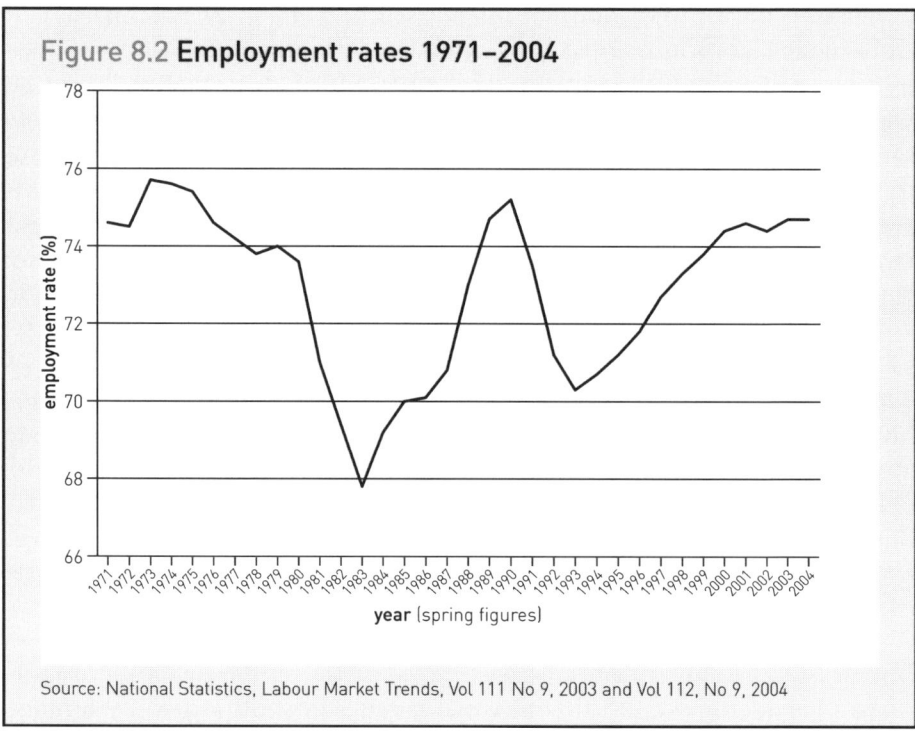

Figure 8.2 **Employment rates 1971–2004**

Source: National Statistics, Labour Market Trends, Vol 111 No 9, 2003 and Vol 112, No 9, 2004

emphasised those who were 'economically inactive' as well as those who counted as 'unemployed' under international definitions because they were actively looking for work. By the end of its first term the government had formalised explicit Public Service Agreement targets aimed at raising employment overall and for a number of key target groups. What it had not yet done was set out a measurable target for what it would mean to achieve 'full employment'.

Improving retention and progression in the labour market

From an early point, one criticism of the New Deals was that they were too focussed on getting participants into a job – any job – regardless of how long that job was likely to last or whether it offered any chance of progression to a better position in the labour market. This led to some focus in policy debates on how the state might improve both retention in employment and further progression in the labour market.

Securing 'fairer outcomes' in the labour market

The government's best response to the allegation that it was too focussed on securing any kind of job for the unemployed was the strong emphasis it placed on eliminating the worst aspects of low pay and reducing in-work poverty. It was also committed to tackling various forms of discrimination in the labour market. It was not, however, obviously committed to reducing the high levels of wage *inequality* it had inherited or tackling the gender pay gap.

Improving the quality of working life

The government was interested in what went on in the workplace, in terms of the quality of day-to-day working life as experienced by employees. It was also very interested in the range of issues relating to work-life balance that had risen up the political agenda during the 1990s.

Keeping business sweet and satisfying the labour movement

It is important not to forget the political context facing the Labour government. It had invested a great deal of capital in establishing and maintaining a good working relationship with business. Indeed, the ippr's other pre-1997 Commission – on Public Policy and British Business – was explicitly geared to this political end. At the same time, the government had to satisfy the expectations of a labour movement battered by two severe recessions and a raft of legislation that had placed restrictions on the role of the trade unions. Squaring this political circle was always going to be tough.

If the wording used to describe some of these objectives seems a little vague, this is in part a reflection of how genuinely difficult it is to define a subjective concept like the 'quality of working life' in a rigorous and measurable manner (see also Edwards and Burkitt, 2001). However, defining *full employment* in a measurable way is something policy makers should be able to do. One such attempt managed to encompass prospects for progression in work and the elimination of in-work poverty, as well as the aspiration that 'Everyone who wants to work can quickly find a job (and) no groups are excluded from the labour market' (Mulgan, 2000). This formulation echoes that of economists in recognising that in a dynamic labour market you will always have a minimum level of 'frictional' unemployment reflecting people changing jobs and spending the optimal time searching for their next best employment opportunity.[1] However, it also adds an important focus on the exclusion of groups from the labour market.

What this government had not done until recently was tell us what actual unemployment and employment rates would constitute full employment. It used the excuse that the labour market had changed so much since the post-war period of full employment that old measures had been rendered redundant, an assertion that should be questioned. Fortunately, statisticians have recreated time-series of unemployment and employment based on current definitions (Figures 8.1 and 8.2) which show that in the early to mid-1970s the unemployment rate was about four per cent, which seems a reasonable benchmark for full employment. Nearly seventy-six per cent of the working age population was in employment at this time. In mid-2004 the employment-population ratio was a little under seventy-five per cent and the unemployment rate a little under five per cent, leading to the

1 One interesting issue for the child poverty debate is whether there might be an analogous 'frictional' level of child poverty that would reflect the temporary movement of households into and out of poverty. This would be the minimum level of child poverty at which the government's flagship target could aim, reflecting the common sense notion that a zero child poverty rate is as unrealistic as a zero unemployment rate.

important conclusion that Britain was still some way off full employment and still below previous post-war peaks. Moreover, some other OECD economies sustained employment rates approaching eighty per cent in the early 2000s as did tighter labour markets in the south of England. Making significant inroads into economic inactivity would seem to require aiming for a similar employment rate for the UK as a whole and importantly in the autumn of 2004 the government began to explicitly refer to an eighty per cent employment rate as representing a benchmark for full employment. An employment rate of at least seventy-five per cent in each region would also seem to be the minimum necessary to pull less advantaged groups back into the labour market in significant numbers.

The government would also claim that it had a very clear assignment of policy instruments to achieve the objectives set out above.

Macroeconomic policy geared to stability
One of the government's proudest boasts is the generally good performance of the UK economy relative both to Britain's recent past and other major OECD economies. They would ascribe this to the monetary and fiscal policy framework put in place after 1997, though it really takes nothing away from the government's achievement to note that this has been built on a framework put in place by the previous government after 1992.

Active labour market policies
The various New Deals are heralded as great success stories, and their impact is discussed further below. Key features were built on successful programmes that were running before 1997, as well as borrowing from both US and Scandinavian experience. It is the setting up of an integrated employment service in the form of Jobcentre Plus that might be one of the government's most significant achievements looking ahead. The New Deals have been inexpensive, with gross annual costs of just £600 million in 2003–4, and in an international context the UK spends less on such policies than most other OECD countries, though of course this tells us nothing about their effectiveness.

Education and training
Famously the Prime Minister's top three priorities, in practice training programmes specifically aimed at disadvantaged jobseekers have played less of a role than active labour market policies geared to helping people move directly into work. This tension between a 'job first' approach and a 'human capital' approach has been a source of policy debate, here and in the US. In particular, the elimination of in-work poverty would seem to require measures that help improve participants' hourly earnings and not just move them into work of any kind. However, the effectiveness of these different approaches is in the end an empirical matter.

Financial incentives

More generous in-work and out-of-work benefits and tax credits aimed primarily at families with children were designed to serve the dual purpose of directly redistributing income to lower income households, while also sharpening incentives to work (though whether they have achieved the latter is unclear, as we discuss below). A national minimum wage was consciously introduced at a modest level to remove the worst features of low pay and further sharpen incentives to work without causing significant job loss.

Labour market regulation

The government also consciously strove to strike a balance in its approach to regulating the labour market between providing more rights and security for employees, and maintaining those elements of 'flexibility' in the labour market that were seen as desirable. Needless to say, striking the balance here and with respect to the minimum wage was central to holding the political ring between business and the labour movement.

A notable absence from this list of policy instruments is any mention of a regional policy designed to raise employment in the less advantaged regions, a point we will come back to.

Of course, setting out the government's policy objectives and instruments in this rational way might suggest the unfolding of a grand plan that was clear to all in 1997. In practice, any government's detailed approach to any major issue evolves pragmatically, even if based on some notion of what is to be achieved and how. The key questions are whether, since 1997, this strategy has contributed to a more socially just set of labour market outcomes and, equally important, where policy might go next?

The government has always faced some strategic choices, most importantly in relation to the emphasis to be given to the four different objectives for the labour market outlined above. The successful introduction of the minimum wage has allowed the government to dismiss the crudest exposition of the trade-off between the level of wages and levels of employment at the bottom end of the labour market, even if at some point that trade-off must exist. Importantly, the capacity of Jobcentre Plus to implement more than one key objective at a time has set up a further potential trade-off between the 'tackling inactivity' and 'promoting progression' agendas that would not have been identified in 1997. This strategic choice faces the government as acutely at the end of its second term in office as it did at the end of its first. It is this potential strategic choice that we primarily focus on in this chapter, with only some limited discussion of the objectives of securing fairer outcomes in the labour market and a better quality of working life.

The evolving labour market

An alien looking at the trends in employment and unemployment in Figures 8.1 and 8.2 might struggle to see an obvious break after 1997 associated with a change in government. Labour inherited a recovering economy in 1997 and that recovery has continued and matured. The key challenge for analysts as always is to establish the counter-factual, what would have happened without the specific policies introduced by this government and how much impact they have had? This is not exactly straightforward, though an attempt is made below.

It is worth setting out some further context in terms of the structure of the labour market and how it has been evolving. Looking at employment patterns by household should give us a better indication of how changes in employment might impact on household incomes (Figure 8.3). The proportion of all working-age households where no adults are in work has fallen by about two-and-a-half percentage points over the decade since 1994, though the proportion of households where all adults are in work has risen by five-and-a-half percentage points over the same period. The proportion of children living in workless households has fallen by a fifth over the decade, but still stood at sixteen per cent in 2004. This is one aspect of the *polarisation* of labour market opportunities that is of concern to those worried about the labour market's contribution to pov-

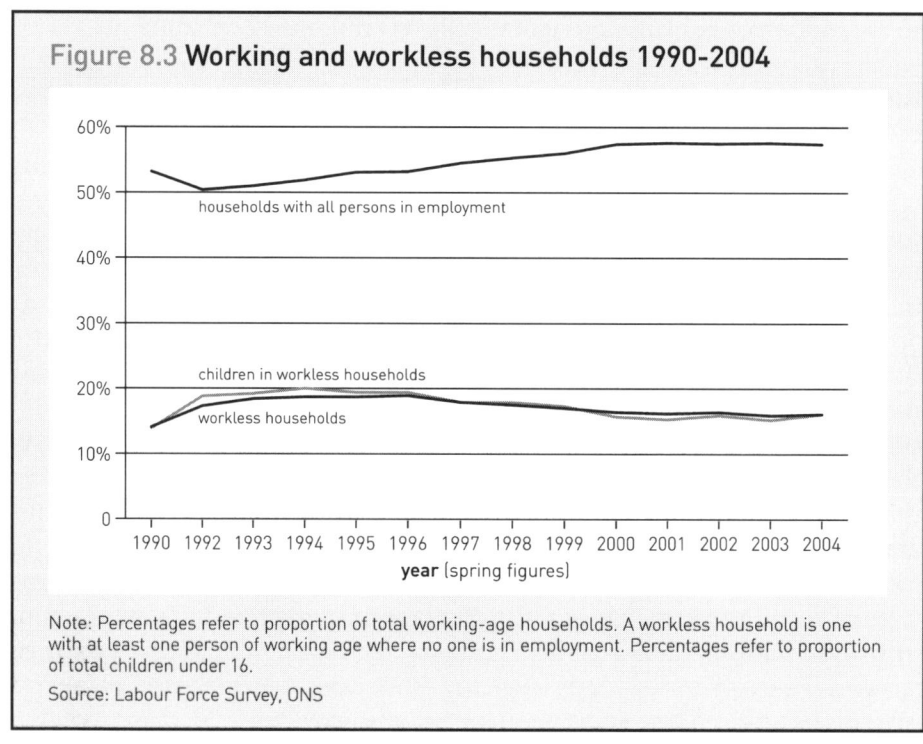

Figure 8.3 **Working and workless households 1990-2004**

households with all persons in employment

children in workless households

workless households

year (spring figures)

Note: Percentages refer to proportion of total working-age households. A workless household is one with at least one person of working age where no one is in employment. Percentages refer to proportion of total children under 16.

Source: Labour Force Survey, ONS

erty, inequality and the achievement of social justice (see also Gregg and Wadsworth, 2003a).

Another aspect of the polarisation debate focuses on the declining share of skilled manual jobs through the 1980s and 1990s and clerical and secretarial jobs in the 1990s (Table 8.1). Less skilled operative and elementary jobs have also seen their share decline. Net growth in employment has come at both ends of the labour market, with a significant increase in managerial, professional and technical jobs but also a rising share of the less well paid personal service and sales occupations. However, overall, two-thirds of the net increase has come in the form of well paid jobs requiring significant qualifications and experience – the British labour market has not been generating disproportionately low-skilled, low-paid work.

Table 8.1 **Changes in the occupational structure of employment in the UK, 1982–2002**

	% of total employment		
	1982	1992	2002
1. Managers and senior officials	10.7	12.6	14.9
2. Professional	8.0	9.4	11.3
3. Associate professional and technical	9.6	11.3	14.0
'Higher occupations'	**28.3**	**33.3**	**40.2**
4. Admin/Clerical/Secretarial	15.5	15.8	13.2
5. Skilled trades	17.0	14.6	11.4
'Intermediate occupations'	**32.5**	**30.4**	**24.6**
6. Personal services	3.7	4.9	7.3
7. Sales/Customer services	6.1	6.7	7.9
8. Transport and machine operatives	11.8	9.7	8.4
9. Elementary occupations	17.7	15.0	11.6
'Lower occupations'	**39.3**	**36.3**	**35.2**

Source: CE/IER estimates, SOC 2000

In terms of the impact of these changes on people's life chances over the generations, the sons and daughters of clerical and skilled manual workers appear to be going off to higher education to fill the growing ranks of those at the top end of the labour market. The continuing worries relate to the bottom end of the labour market and the changes in the skills required and the attractiveness of jobs in the personal services compared with less skilled manual jobs. There is, however, one puzzle to resolve: this polarisation in the labour market was associated with widening wage inequality

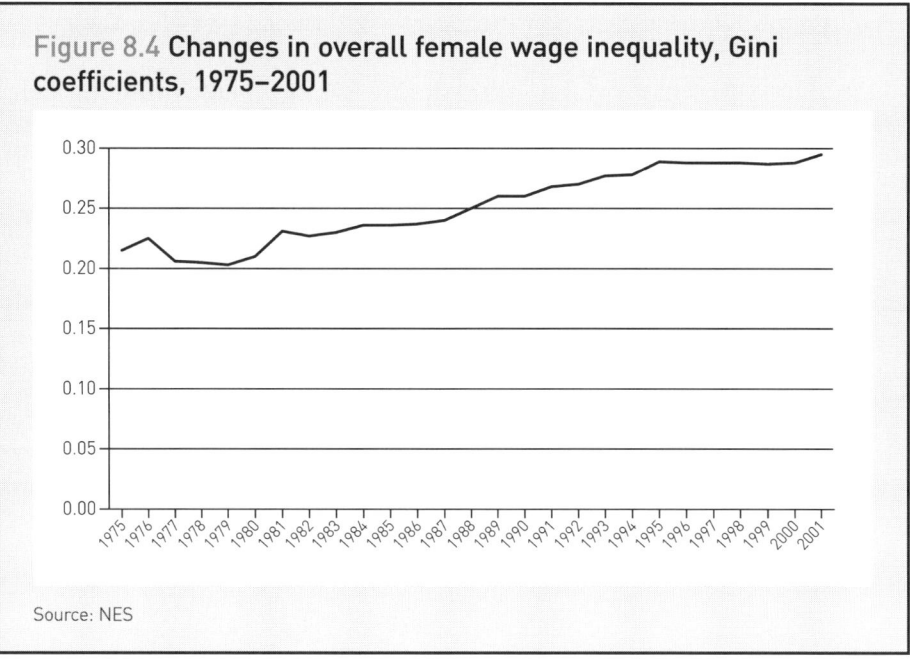

Figure 8.4 **Changes in overall female wage inequality, Gini coefficients, 1975–2001**

Source: NES

in the 1980s and early 1990s, but the same broad pattern of polarisation continued through the rest of the 1990s when the growth in wage inequality slowed down significantly.

Clearly, the trends in wage inequality are of critical importance to debates on social justice. There are a number of data sources to draw on with different strengths and weaknesses, but Figure 8.4 uses data on hourly wages from the New Earnings Survey, focussing on the trends for women, though the trends for men are not wholly dissimilar (for discussion see Machin, 2003). Wage inequality in the UK labour market rose sharply from the late 1970s to the early 1990s. However, since the mid-1990s this growth has been much tempered. Data from the Labour Force Survey also shows a great deal of stability between 1996 and 2001 in the wage premiums attached to the holding of particular qualifications following a period in the 1980s when the better qualified pulled ahead in terms of their wages (Sianesi, 2003). These trends mirror those discussed in the chapter in this report by Goodman, Shaw and Shephard which shows that underlying inequality in gross (original or market) household income has not changed much over the period 1996–7 to 2002–3.

It is worth emphasising these contrasts between the experience of the 1990s and the 1980s. Much comment on the labour market – including that contained in the 1994 Commission on Social Justice – has a decidedly 'trotskyist' feel to it, asserting that the labour market is in the grip of some form of permanent revolution. In part this is based on false notions of what the labour market was supposed to have looked like in the post-war period when female labour force participation and part-time employment were already rising rapidly and most people did *not* have access to jobs for life.

The break in trend from the early 1990s – that is the steady improvement in employment and the slowing down of the growth in wage inequality – poses a real challenge to labour market analysts. The adverse trends in wage inequality from the late 1970s to the early 1990s were put down to a range of interwoven factors:

- the shock of two sharp recessions in the early 1980s and early 1990s

- the shift in demand away from the less skilled as a result of technological change and greater international competition

- institutional changes, including the decline of the trade unions and collective bargaining, the end of incomes policies and the phasing out of minimum wage protection

- and, at the risk of sounding like a soft sociologist, attitudinal changes that made very high pay awards at the top end of the labour market more acceptable and supported the institutional changes that undermined wages at the bottom end.

By the time of the 1994 Commission on Social Justice there was no wholly convincing or complete explanation of the trends towards more unequal rewards in the labour market. Unfortunately, this uncertainty was not reflected in the Commission's report. The fact that no-one predicted the break in trend from about that point on and that indeed the existence of that break in trend is only just being fully recognised should humble us further.

Looking back at the factors listed above, the first obvious puzzle is why continuous technological change and further 'globalisation' has been associated with one set of outcomes for market inequality in the 1980s and a different set from the mid-1990s? The avoidance of further catastrophic shocks to employment after the early 1990s recession must count for something. The decline in coverage of the unions and collective bargaining in the UK slowed down from the mid-1990s, but on the other hand, the wage premium that results from trade union membership still appears to have declined over the 1990s and especially for the less well qualified. We now have a national minimum wage, but the change in trend pre-dates its introduction and it is set at too modest a level to make much of a contribution. Sharp improvements in educational attainment have gradually fed through to improve the stock of qualifications in the labour market and this must help explain some of the change in trend. However, it is not obvious that attitudes have changed to render further increases in inequality somehow less acceptable. In short, we still do not have a wholly convincing or complete explanation of these trends. Of course this makes public policy making all the more difficult.

A great deal had been learned before 1997 about the kinds of interventions that appeared to be most cost-effective in helping the workless to move into employment. Drawing on UK experience and some lessons from the US and Scandinavia, the emphasis has been on creating a unified employment and benefit service for the working age population. At the heart of Jobcentre Plus is the model of the personal adviser helping individuals to search more effectively for work and offering incentives and removing barriers to help ease the path into employment – very consciously a work-first model. It should be stressed that evaluations of the effectiveness of different active labour market programmes available at the time would have pushed policy in this direction (Robinson, 2000).

Although the original headline target group for the New Deal was the young long-term unemployed, the government had by 2000 moved clearly towards targeting key groups suffering not just from high unemployment, but from high levels of economic inactivity. A rising economic tide tends to lift most boats, so the steady economic recovery from the early 1990s would have been expected to raise employment rates even for these relatively excluded groups. Figure 8.5 shows employment rates for the over-50s and for lone parents rising steadily from 1993 and at a faster rate than the overall rate, so that the gap between the employment rates of these groups and the

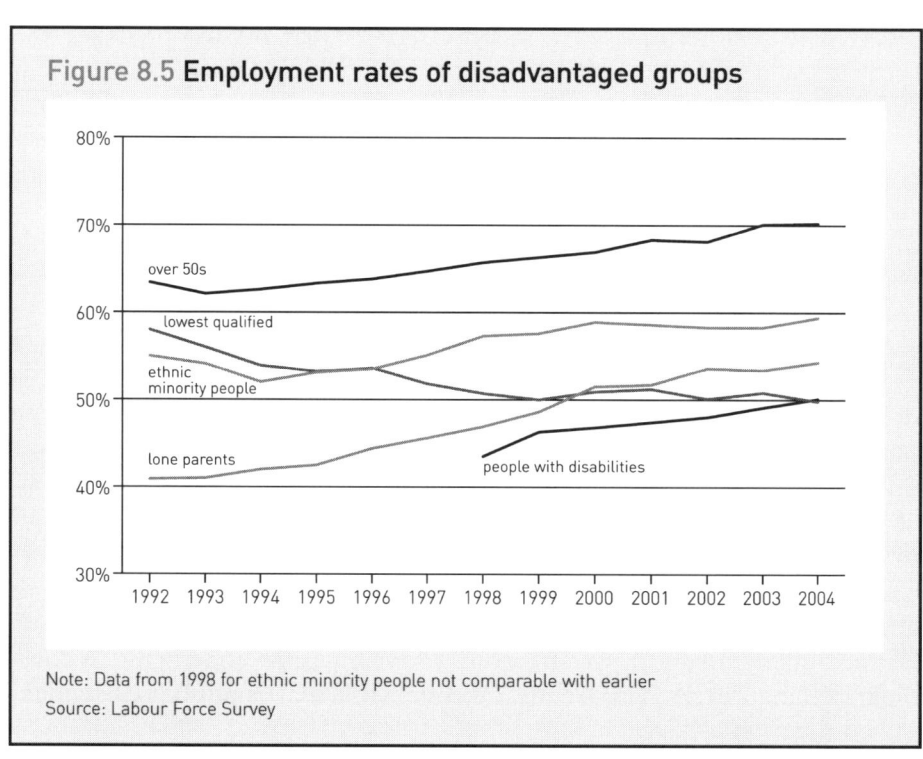

Figure 8.5 **Employment rates of disadvantaged groups**

Note: Data from 1998 for ethnic minority people not comparable with earlier
Source: Labour Force Survey

overall employment rate has narrowed. A shorter but consistent time series for people with disabilities shows their employment rate rising since 1998 and also at a faster rate than the overall rate. However, more people are identifying themselves as having a disability so the overall size of this excluded group continues to pose concerns (see Stanley and Regan, 2003 for further discussion). The employment rate for ethnic minority people has also risen since 1994, but at a pace similar to the overall rate. However, employment rates for the lowest qualified have not recovered, though this partly reflects a compositional effect as this group has gradually got older on average. This makes the point of course that these different groups overlap significantly. Older people with a disability and lacking qualifications, for example, might be expected to face some of the most significant barriers to employment.

Taking each group separately, people with disabilities constitute the largest single category along with the lowest qualified, and with worklessness amongst both groups very strongly concentrated regionally (see Adams, Robinson and Vigor, 2003). An overall employment rate in excess of seventy-five per cent appears to be required in a labour market to lift the demand for the less skilled (Gregg and Wadsworth, 2003b). This reinforces the concern that the spatial dimension of employment had been neglected, but even here the government has begun to show more interest, emphasising the importance of reducing inactivity, especially related to disability, as key to reducing regional disparities in prosperity.

Issues relating to gender are also rather hidden within these excluded groups: lone parents are of course disproportionately women; employment rates are especially low for women from some Asian communities; rates of reported disability amongst women of working age are similar to rates amongst men.

To give an indication of the scale of the challenge that remains in tackling unemployment and inactivity, employment rates for all these excluded groups still lag between five and twenty-five percentage points behind the overall rate. Raising the employment rate of people with disabilities to the overall employment rate would require an increase in employment of 1.8 million, about equivalent to the entire increase in employment from 1997 to 2004. It is worth emphasising this point because in some circles, including for example the DTI, one sometimes hears musing along the lines of 'employment – been there, solved that', with the implication that policy makers can move onto other agendas relating to productivity or quality of working life. The scale of the challenge is also worth emphasising as background to the strategic choices that still face the government.

What has been learned from evaluations of the New Deals and the tax and benefit changes introduced to sharpen work incentives? The evaluation literature is voluminous, and summarising it in a paragraph or two is not easy. The combination of the New Deal for lone parents and tax/benefit changes may have increased the employment rate of lone parents by about five percentage points or by 80,000 between 1998 and 2002 (Gregg and Harkness, 2003). As the authors emphasise, this was in the context of a programme where participation was 'voluntary' and despite generous increases in benefits for those families where the lone parent is not in employment. They also point out, however, that the remaining population of non-employed lone parents is less skilled and concentrated in rented housing, suggesting further significant gains in employment might be more difficult.

The aggregate impact of the flagship New Deal for Young People has been to raise employment amongst the target group by about 17,000 a year, though the impact may be bigger if the programme has reduced wage pressure by turning unemployed 'outsiders' into 'insiders' (Blundell *et al.*, 2003). As the authors emphasise this impact does not amount to a dramatic transformation of the youth labour market, though given the modest gross costs of the scheme, it offers reasonably good value-for-money. The new deal for the over fifties has not been evaluated in the same rigorous fashion, but has probably played little role in the significant increase in employment that has taken place for this group (Disney and Hawkes, 2003).

The overall impact of the government's tax and benefit reforms on work incentives is not completely straightforward (Brewer and Shephard, 2004). These reforms have raised the incomes of both families with children where one or more adults are in work and families where the adults are out of work. Lone parents face improved incentives to work, but the incentives to work for second earners in two-adult households have on average worsened. Overall incentives have improved for workless households but not for two-earner households.

The government's active labour market policies and its tax and benefit changes have made a contribution to reducing unemployment and increasing employment for the target groups and in the overall labour market. Contrary to government propaganda, the scale of the effects is to be measured in the tens rather than the hundreds of thousands, but in contrast to Opposition propaganda these policies have definitely not been a waste of resources.

In terms of going forward, as already indicated, the scale of the challenge remains significant. In this context the observation that the Jobcentre Plus network, first launched in October 2001, will not be fully in place until 2006 is germane. It is a useful rule of thumb that if policy makers advocate significant administrative changes as a necessary component of any policy, they should factor in half a decade for those changes to bed down. The staff in jobcentres are having to concentrate more and more of their attention on inactive groups that have not traditionally been the main clients for their services, focussing attention on the balance of skills and staffing within the agency. In many ways Jobcentre Plus exemplifies the challenges facing the public services, of how to offer more 'personalised' services and the workforce implications this involves, how to make funding more sensitive to variations in need across the country, and how to reconcile local managerial autonomy with the need to meet national targets.

The approach of Jobcentre Plus so far has been primarily based on the 'work-first' model, with limited attempts to build up participants' 'human capital'. Given that this approach was based in part on the experience of US programmes, a comprehensive review of the impact of US welfare-to-work programmes published in 2004 is salutary (Greenberg *et al.*, 2004). This found that the positive impact of such programmes could persist for up to five to six years, but that the impact of the work-first approach was much greater than the human capital approach even after this period of time. The UK government does appear to have been doing what works based on the evaluation evidence available in 1997 and in 2004. The impact of training programmes emphasising the human capital approach in the UK is discussed below.

Improving retention and progression

The perceived lack of attention to helping people to secure jobs that may last for a reasonable period of time and helping people to progress to better positions in the labour market will remain a persistent criticism of current policy. Policy makers in 1997 were aware of the problem of a substantial minority of the British workforce – around five to ten per cent – who spent their entire lives in a cycle of disadvantage moving between low paid jobs, often with spells of unemployment and inactivity in between (Meadows, 1999). These repeated returns to benefit were known to have scarring effects on individuals' future employment prospects. The problem was that, unlike the experience with active labour market policies that the New Deals might build on, the evidence on what worked in improving retention and progression was sparse.

Post-employment support services can build on the services already offered to participants in existing employment programmes, effectively offering a follow-up service to help people keep the jobs the employment services have helped them secure and also perhaps to progress to better jobs. They can also target people already in low paid employment. These services can offer help with childcare, transport or specific financial incentives to keep people in work. They can also offer training programmes designed to enhance participants' human capital to help them gain a better job. At the heart of such interventions is the same personal adviser model that has been at the centre of existing employment programmes, the idea being of course that the same adviser can continue to maintain contact with those people who they have placed in work.

There are examples of post-employment services in North America that have been evaluated, but not often in the same rigorous fashion as mainstream employment programmes (Kellard *et al.*, 2002). The evaluation evidence suggests that financial incentives may improve job retention rates at least in the short-run, with limited, less robust evidence that assistance with transport, employer-provided childcare, financial assistance to help deal with domestic emergencies, job coaching and mentoring programmes and skills training may also help. A key pointer as to why such programmes might face difficulties lies in the observation that personal advisers are often overwhelmed by their caseload and that the pressure to help those clients still looking for a job limits the time and resources available for post-employment support.

The response of the UK government has been to launch an ambitious Employment Retention and Advancement (ERA) Demonstration project that will be evaluated using the rigorous random assignment methods characteristic of the best US evaluations. It is targeted at those eligible for the New Deal for the over twenty-five age group and those volunteering for the New Deal for Lone Parents, as well as lone parents on Working Tax Credit (WTC) working part-time in low paid jobs. For the two New Deal groups help will start before they enter employment; for the WTC group after they have started working. There will be one-to-one support for each participant from a dedicated Advancement Support Advisor for up to two years after someone has entered employment, with financial incentives to encourage retention in full-time work and to support approved education or training. Quite consciously, the ERA Demonstration is being piloted with up to 27,000 individuals and with no plans at the outset to roll it out on a national scale before the results of the evaluation are known, which will be from about 2006–7 onwards. Indeed, for a government notorious for announcing every single initiative many times over, the almost subliminal status of this initiative is striking.

If this really is the ultimate demonstration of evidence-based policy making, the government has effectively given itself most of the period of a third term in office to see whether such post-employment services are effective, before any attempt to roll them out. This may be based on a conscious calculation that Jobcentre Plus will in the meantime have its hands full with reducing inactivity amongst the key target groups. Faced with the strategic choice of using the limited capacity of the employment services to deal with either inactivity on the one hand or retention and progression on the other, the government has prioritised the former.

The evidence base on the effectiveness of training programmes for the adult workless may or may not have influenced this decision. Of the three types of training offered under the Work-Based Learning for Adults (WBLA) programme, one had no impact on employment, a second accelerated entry into work but had no long-term effects on employment, and the third significantly increased the chances of working thirty hours or more (Anderson *et al.*, 2004). None of the types of training had any impact on wages, suggesting no enhancement of human capital. These conclusions mirror the results of a set of disappointing evaluations of such training programmes going back to the 1980s (Robinson, 2000). We have some idea then of what appears *not* to work and the results of these UK evaluations are no more favourable to the human capital approach than the US evaluations.

One of the government's key flagship skills initiatives, the Employer Training Pilots (ETPs), offers incentives for workplace based training aimed at getting participants their first level 2 qualification, seen as the minimum level necessary for people to be able to make some progression in the labour market. Initial evaluation suggested good take-up but with a heavy concentration in certain sectors and especially the care sector (Hillage and Mitchell, 2003). However, take-up is only a preliminary indication of programme success. The qualifications attained and most importantly the progression made in the labour market as measured by earnings will be the key indicators of success. Participants are almost all working towards level 2 NVQs, which is a little worrying as research has suggested these qualifications have at best no impact on earnings and may even have a negative impact. However, the most recent research suggests that for women working in the health and social care sector, obtaining a level 2 NVQ does yield a significantly higher wage (Dearden *et al.*, 2004). This makes the important point that the type of qualification attained by participants on training programmes matters as does the role played by those qualifications in particular sectors of the economy. Not all qualifications are the same in terms of their purchase in the labour market. The announcement in the December 2004 Pre-Budget Report that a National Employer Training Programme based on the ETPs would be rolled out from 2006–7 without knowing the impact of the pilots on participants' progress in the labour market does *not* show a government truly committed to evidence-based policy making, where the focus should be on outcomes not take-up.

Fairer outcomes

The successful introduction of the national minimum wage (at a relatively modest level) was one of the significant early achievements of the government, not least because employers were brought around to support its introduction. Its value relative to average earnings has been increased modestly since its introduction and its coverage is being extended to sixteen and seventeen year olds. And importantly, employers remain on board, even if parts of the labour movement and some other observers believe the government remains too cautious. The other pressure requiring this government to act, in much the same way as the previous government, comes from the need to meet EU Directives relating to employment rights, especially in relation to working time and in relation to countering discrimination.

The government therefore faces three sets of pressures, from employers, the labour movement and the EU. To a significant extent its approach to employment regulation reflects how it balances those pressures. There has been some loose talk about renewed forms of 'social partnership'. At a practical level this has involved some useful, modest, initiatives such as the Union Learning Fund. However, there can be no pretence that what is envisaged is anything along the lines of northern European forms of partnership. More cynically it might be viewed as a strategy of 'wine and canapés' to replace 'beer and sandwiches' as a device for squaring competing political interests.

If the government has a strategy to secure 'fairer outcomes' then it relies on many of the same instruments designed to reduce unemployment and inactivity: benefits, tax credits and the minimum wage to sharpen incentives and reduce in-work poverty; measures to tackle discrimination; and education and training to improve human capital. As already discussed, the term 'fairer outcomes' does not yet encompass an explicit objective of tackling overall wage inequality or the gender wage gap, other than through the contribution made by the policy instruments discussed above. If the comparatively high levels of wage inequality and the large gender pay gap in the UK are in some large part a function of institutional factors including relatively low levels of unionisation and collective bargaining, it is definitely not part of the government's agenda to borrow this aspect of the Scandinavian model.

Quality of working life

A random sample of the speeches, seminars or publications of the policy-making establishment might lead one to believe that excessive working hours, childcare costs and general unhappiness amongst the professional classes was one of the most pressing problems facing the UK. Clearly the government believes that quality of working life issues are bound to rise up the political agenda in the context of a broadly affluent population in a labour market closer to full employment. The challenge for progressives is to balance this set of issues against the unresolved problems of high levels of economic inactivity, poor opportunities for progression at the lower end of the labour market, and continued inequality.

One obvious way forward for those committed to social justice is to view quality of working life issues from the point of view of those at the lower end of the labour market. This could help us to think through our priorities in relation, for example, to the issue of employees not working the hours they would like. In autumn 2001, almost three million workers would have accepted less pay to be able to work fewer hours; 2.4 million workers wanted to work longer hours; if everyone had been working the hours they wanted, the total volume of hours worked would have been little altered (Simic, 2002a, 2002b). The contrast between the two groups lies in their distribution: over-employment disproportionately affects managerial

and professional workers and the well paid; under-employment disproportionately affects the lowest occupational groups and the lowest paid. Policy
debates on the other hand, even among progressives, seem to concentrate
on the former group.

Conclusion

A commitment to social justice should always lead policy makers to focus
on those excluded from the labour market and those at the lower end of
the labour market. However, the passion or anger that continuing exclusion and inequality should engender needs to be balanced by a dispassion-
ate assessment of the effectiveness of different policy instruments. One key
observation for progressives to mull over is that there will always be some
jobs at the lower end of the labour market that demand modest skills and
offer lower pay and limited progression. Jobs in the social care sector are
not going to be displaced anytime soon by technology or foreign competition (though migrants might fill some of them).

Two key research challenges are; firstly, to understand better the trends
in wage inequality and that break in trend in the early 1990s and, secondly, to understand what combination of policy instruments will help
bring about a significant reduction in inactivity, especially amongst those
suffering from ill-health or a disability. What might have worked for the
unemployed or lone parents may not work so well for the disabled. Current
initiatives such as the Pathways to Work Pilots may give us some further
clues, but again rigorous evaluations of these pilots will take some time to
become available.

The current government faces four key policy challenges in employment
policy if it secures a third term.

- It has already made the choice to give priority to tackling inactivity
  rather than promoting retention and/or progression. This is the right
  choice, given limitations on the capacity of Jobcentre Plus and the scale
  of the problem of inactivity, but the challenge referred to above, of finding out what works for different client groups, is acute.

- Further reductions in relative poverty, in-work and out-of-work, will
  continue to prove expensive, whatever combination of policy instruments is chosen. The government may be a little less cautious in push-
  ing up the minimum wage, but tax credits and benefits will remain the
  main instrument for improving incomes and sharpening incentives.
  However, after 2006–7 the rate of growth in public spending will fall
  significantly outside of health (and international development). The
  Chancellor has previously found the extra resources for increases in
  credits and benefits at the time of each Budget and Pre-Budget Report,
  but the scope for such pragmatism will be limited in a harsher fiscal

environment. In this context the conclusion by Brewer (2005) that up to two billion pounds more will be required each and every year to secure progress towards halving child poverty by 2010, and more if work incentives are to be sharpened, is salutary to say the least.

- Those who advocate more of a human capital approach need to be clear about what skills/qualifications they think will give participants greater purchase in the labour market. When education ministers talk so much about 'personalised' learning in schools, the current emphasis in adult learning on offering an undifferentiated diet of level 2 NVQs is very problematic. There is a fundamental difference between a system driven by the choices of individual adults, with those choices supported by adequate funding, and a system driven by planning bodies with funding going via the employer, which discussion about a vague 'new deal for skills' completely fails to address.

- The government's political capital with employers will need to be used up in advancing further leave entitlements for parents and carers of adults after 2006, which means avoiding conflict in other areas. This will leave the government subject to criticism from the unions and others that it is not doing enough to 'compel' employers in other areas, such as training.

The past decade has seen significant improvements in labour market outcomes, but in the next decade we will need to see further in-roads into inactivity and poverty if the goals of social justice are to be further advanced.

References

Adams, J, Robinson, P. and Vigor, A. (2003) *A New Regional Policy for the UK* ippr

Anderson, T., Dorsett, R., Hales, J., Lissenburgh, S., Pires, C., Smeaton, D., (2004) *Work-based Learning for Adults: An evaluation of labour market effects* Department for Work and Pensions, (March)

Blundell, R., Reed, H., Van Reenen, J. and Shephard, A. (2003) 'The Impact of the New Deal on the Labour Market: A four-year assessment' in Dickens, R., Gregg P. and Wadsworth, J. (eds.) *The Labour Market under New Labour* Palgrave Macmillan

Brewer, M. and Shephard, A. (2004) *Has Labour Made Work Pay?* Institute for Fiscal Studies/Joseph Rowntree Foundation

Brewer, M. (2005), 'Maintaining Momentum in Tackling Child Poverty' in Delorenzi, S, Reed, J. and Robinson, P. (eds.) *Promoting Social Mobility and Life Chances: Maintaining Momentum* ippr

Burchardt, T. (2004) 'Just Happiness? Subjective well-being and social policy' unpublished paper, CASE/LSE

Commission on Social Justice (1994) *Social Justice: Strategies for national renewal* ippr

Commission on Public Policy and British Business (1997) *Promoting Prosperity: A business agenda for Britain* ippr

Dearden, L, McGranahan, L. and Sianesi, B. (2004) 'An in-depth analysis of the returns to national vocational qualifications obtained at level 2' Discussion Paper, Centre for the Economics of Education

Department for Work and Pensions (2004) 'Building on New Deal: Local solutions meeting individual needs' Preliminary Paper, DWP

Department for Work and Pensions/Office for National Statistics (2004) *Households below average income, 1994–5 to 2002–3* DWP/ONS

Disney, R. and Hawkes, D. (2003) 'Why has employment recently risen among older workers in Britain?' in Dickens, R., Gregg P. and Wadsworth, J. (eds.) *The Labour Market under New Labour* Palgrave Macmillan

Di Tella, R., MacCulloch R.J. and Oswald A.J. (2002) 'The Macroeconomics of Happiness' Centre for Economic Performance/Oxford University Discussion Paper (July)

Edwards, L. and Burkitt, N. (2001), 'Wanting more from work? Aspirations and expectations of work' in Burkitt, N. (ed.) *A Life's Work: Achieving full and fulfilling employment* ippr

Goodman, A., Shaw, J. and Shephard, A. (2005) 'Understanding recent trends in income inequality' in Delorenzi, S, Reed, J. and Robinson, P. (eds.) *Promoting Social Mobility and Life Chances: Maintaining momentum* ippr 2005

Greenberg, D., Ashworth, K., Cebulla, A. and Walker, R. (2004) 'Do welfare to work programmes work for long' *Fiscal Studies* 25 (1):27-54

Gregg, P. and Harkness, S. (2003) 'Welfare reform and the employment of lone parents' in Dickens, R., Gregg, P. and Wadsworth, J. (eds) *The Labour Market Under New Labour* Palgrave Macmillan

Gregg, P. and Wadsworth, J. (2003a) 'Workless households and the recovery' in Dickens, R., Gregg P. and Wadsworth, J. (eds.) *The Labour Market under New Labour* Palgrave Macmillan

Gregg, P. and Wadsworth, J. (2003b) 'Labour market prospects of less skilled workers over the recovery' in Dickens, R., Gregg, P. and Wadsworth, J. (eds.) *The Labour Market under New Labour* Palgrave Macmillan

Hillage, J and Mitchell, H. (2003) *Employer Training Pilots: First year evaluation report* Institute for Employment Studies for the DfES/HMT/LSC

Kellard, K., Adelman, L, Cebulla, A. and Heaver, C. (2002) *From Job Seekers to Job Keepers: Job retention, advancement and the role of in-work support programmes* Centre for Research on Social Policy, Loughborough University for the Department for Work and Pensions

Machin, S. (2003) 'Wage Inequality since 1975' in Dickens, R., Gregg, P. and Wadsworth, J. (eds.) *The Labour Market under New Labour* Palgrave Macmillan

Meadows, P. (1999) *The Flexible Labour Market: Implications for pension provision* National Association of Pension Funds

Mulgan, G. (2000), 'Full Employment: the UK' in Muet, P.A., Pisani-Ferry, J., Mulgan, G. and Layard, R. *Achieving Full Employment* Policy Network

Robinson, P. (2000) 'Active Labour Market Policies: A case of evidence based policy making?' *Oxford Review of Economic Policy* 16(1):13-26 OUP

Sianesi, B. (2003) 'Returns to Education: A non-technical summary of CEE work and policy discussion' *mimeo* IFS and Centre for the Economics of Education (June)

Simic, M. (2002a) 'Underemployment and Overemployment in the UK' *Labour Market Trends* 110(8):399-414 (August)

Simic, M. (2002b) 'Volume of Underemployment and Overemployment in the UK' *Labour Market Trends* 110 (10):511-522 (October)

Stanley, K. and Regan, S. (2003) *The Missing Million: Supporting disabled people into work* ippr